The ZENBELLY COOKBOOK

An Epicurean's Guide to Paleo Cuisine

written and photographed by Simone Miller

VICTORY BELT PUBLISHING INC.

Las Vegas

For my Grandma:
Strong as an ox, sweet as honey. You're
the winner.

First Published in 2014 by Victory Belt Publishing Inc.

Copyright © Simone Miller

ISBN-13: 978-1-628600-21-6

Printed in the USA

RRD 0114

contents

introduction

You could probably get through life without knowing how to roast a chicken, but the question is, would you want to?

~ Nigella Lawson

Most of my early memories involve food.

Once I was old enough to count and could be trusted with vegetable-picking activities, my mom would send me to our backyard garden to pick tomatoes. She would say, "Simone, please go to the garden and pick me three ripe tomatoes." I would return, ten minutes later, with one tomato and tomato juice all over my face. "Where are the other tomatoes?" she'd ask with a laugh, as if it she didn't know.

I remember eating chopped liver in my aunt's backyard at a summer party, knowing, somehow, that it wasn't something I was supposed to like. None of my friends ate it, that's for sure. But I loved it, just like I loved the pickled herring that my Grandma Loretta fed me every time I visited my grandparents in the Bronx. I stopped liking it at some point, when I was old enough to be grossed out by cold, pickled fish. But I couldn't bring myself to tell her—it made her so happy that I would eat such a thing— and I continued to eat it when I visited. How could I not, when she was so excited to tell me she got my favorite snack? "Simoney! I got you pickled herring!" I would pretend to be grossed out later, on the ride home, but I never really stopped liking the stuff, just the idea of it.

And of course, being the children of an extremely loving and maternal Jewish mom, my brother and I didn't have to do much more than sneeze for there to be a pot of chicken soup bubbling on the stove.

Regardless of my early love for good food, I never wanted to be a chef. In fact, despite working in several restaurants throughout my late teens and twenties, I never even considered making a career of it.

I got my first food job at nineteen, at a small vegetarian cafe in Willimantic, Connecticut. I was in college and didn't for one second think of the job I had making sandwiches and soups and milkshakes as one that would blossom into my career. After all, I was in college, not culinary school. There was a reason for that: I was not going to be a chef. After two and a half years in college without ever settling on a major, I suddenly thought I found my calling: I was going to be a massage therapist. I stopped going to college and enrolled in massage school. I loved it. And I loved being a massage therapist. Until . . . I didn't. For about ten years, I went back and forth between polar opposite jobs. I was either working in spas, wearing all black, listening to Enya, smelling lavender, and communicating in whispers, or I was wearing all white, yelling above the sound of the exhaust fan and death metal, smelling (and smelling like) onions and bacon, and swearing like a sailor. When I got sick of one, I went back to the other. Neither felt quite right.

It wasn't until I moved to California in 2007 that something clicked. Well, a few things, actually:

01 I love to create delicious food that makes people happy.

02 I do not like working in restaurants.

03 I do not like massaging people.

While it's always good to have clarity, I didn't see a solution lurking in my above epiphany. Most chefs get jobs in restaurants, after all, or start their own. And people who do not like massaging people should not be massaging people. So that was undoubtedly out.

At the time, I was working for a sweet family in Marin Country, California, as a personal assistant. The job mostly entailed cooking healthy meals for them, which I loved. When the mom was planning their annual holiday party, she mentioned to me that she wanted to have it catered by someone who was willing to use all (or almost all) organic ingredients. She was having a difficult time finding a caterer who would accommodate the level of quality she was seeking. "I'll do it," I said, without thinking much about the words that were coming out of my mouth. I had catered a family party with my brother, Elijah, years prior, and had worked in a bunch of restaurants, so why not? I was certain that I could pull it off.

And I did, and it was brilliant, and a lightbulb went off. I could cook for people without working in a restaurant, and I could finally throw in the massage towel.

Of course, it wasn't that simple. Shortly after starting my catering business, I had to make major changes in my diet. This wouldn't have been much of an issue if I still worked in a spa or had an office job. But dietary restrictions for a chef might as well be the kiss of death. Feeling like crap all of the time certainly wasn't going to contribute to success on any realm. So now, after much trial, error, and inevitably, denial, I eat 100-percent gluten-free and mostly Paleo, and I have modeled my catering company, Zenbelly, after that.

What is Paleo?

"Paleo" is short for Paleolithic. The premise of this way of eating is to eat the way our ancestors ate, before the agricultural revolution introduced grains, legumes, refined sugar, and dairy.

But let's make one thing abundantly clear: This is *not* a historical reenactment. In fact, the thing I like the least about the Paleo diet happens to be the word *Paleo*. People see it and jump to all kind of false conclusions. Let's just go ahead and debunk a few of my favorites right off the bat.

- **"You have to eat what and how cavemen ate."**

Did they eat chicken? Coconut oil? Almond butter? Perfectly cut six-ounce steaks in plastic-wrapped packages? No. They didn't. Can we? Heck, yes. And we don't have to tackle our dinner wearing a loincloth, either. And thank goodness for that, for I am not an athletic girl.

- **"I could never eat that way! I love food too much!"**

I usually stare blankly at this question, wishing I was wearing my chef coat and ugly clogs, for effect. I'm sorry, you love food too much? And I'm a chef because . . . I don't like food at all? Huh. Weird. Let's clear something up: The Paleo diet is not restrictive. True, it cuts out a lot of convenience foods and, for the most part, bread. But convenience foods are almost always not food at all. I could go into more detail here proving my point, but instead, I wrote a cookbook. Guess what it's full of? Food. It's full of delicious food. You could make every recipe in this book and feed it to someone who has never heard the word *Paleo*, and they will love it.

- **"But meat and fat are bad for you!"**

Because this is a cookbook and not a nutrition textbook, I'm not going to go into all the gory details here. To keep it short and sweet, the above statement is simply false. Factory-farmed meat is not a healthy food because the animals raised in those conditions are fed a diet that they should absolutely not be eating—not to mention the horrific conditions they are forced to live in. Animals that are raised properly and fed a species-appropriate diet, however, are a completely different . . . (wait for it) . . . animal. And in terms of fat: I know it's a difficult concept to swallow, but healthy sources of fat are absolutely vital. In fact, our fear of these nutrient-dense sources over the past fifty-plus years is a large part of why our collective health has landed right in the proverbial crapper. For more complete and science-y information on this topic, I recommend reading *Eat the Yolks* by Liz Wolfe, *Cholesterol Clarity* by Jimmy Moore and Eric C. Westman, *Practical Paleo* by Diane Sanfilippo, *The Paleo Solution* by Robb Wolf, *Your Personal Paleo Code* by Chris Kresser, LAC, and *The Primal Blueprint* by Mark Sisson.

To me, and to many of my wonderful catering clients, blog readers, and friends, eating this way simply means eating real food. It means making delicious balanced meals out of real, unprocessed foods: animals, plants, and healthy fats. And there's a lot of variety, a lot of flavor, and all sorts of gourmet stuff happening when you eat this way.

Why do I eat this way?

The short answer:

I feel better.

The long answer:

I feel way better.

No, but really—my "normal" used to include lethargy, depression, near-constant headaches, brain fog, problem skin, and general malaise. I got migraines regularly. My joints felt achy. I got horrible colds at least twice a year, and they lasted for weeks. My blood sugar was all over the place. When I got hungry (which was often), I felt like a crazy person: I couldn't reason, I felt like I was going to pass out, and I was not nice to the people around me. (Sorry, people!) Basically, I just didn't feel good. I thought there was something wrong with me; maybe I had a thyroid issue, or a lymph issue, or worse. It was very scary to feel generally unwell and not know what was causing it.

In 2008, I had a food allergy test done at my chiropractor's office after putting it off for months out of fear of the inevitable—I was going to have to change how I ate. The results were no big shocker, and they shone a big ol' light on what I had known deep down for quite some time: Gluten is not my friend.

But we can still be acquaintances, right? Right?! Wrong.

After I eliminated gluten from my diet entirely, there was no going back. Believe me, I tried. Once my body adjusted to being gluten-free, my sensitivity to gluten became more severe. Now, if I accidently ingest gluten when I'm out to eat, I'm greeted the next morning with a migraine-esque headache that lasts two to three days, brain fog, and fatigue. It's safe to say that I'm also pretty cranky during a gluten hangover. There is nothing worth eating that results in all of that. And you should know: I love (LOVE) bagels.

Let's take a step back and look at the timing of all of this. After years of trying to love being a massage therapist, I had rediscovered my love for feeding people. I was in the process of starting a catering business, and not being able to eat an ingredient that is in almost everything was sure to make owning and operating a catering business a challenge. I don't follow recipes; I taste as I go. I cannot serve people food that I haven't tasted and perfected.

So I had a decision to make: I could call it quits and find a new line of work (again), or I could make my catering company 100-percent gluten-free.

I chose the latter, and I can honestly say that it was the best decision I've made for my career, my health, and my clients.

Like many people who go gluten-free, I dove head first into recreating old favorites. I perfected as many gluten-free baked goods as I could. I reveled in the gluten-free section of my grocery store. Gluten-free breads and pastas became staples in my diet. In short, I ate a bunch of crap. While I felt better with my new gluten-free lifestyle, I still didn't feel great. I was thirty and didn't have any medical conditions. Shouldn't I feel great?

I'm not sure where I first heard about Paleo, but my first impression of it, admittedly, wasn't great. Like many people who only hear and see the short story, I saw meat, more meat, and a little bit of veggies. And meat. Don't get me wrong, after seven-plus very unhealthy and unsatisfying years of being a vegetarian, I had embraced my carnivore roots wholeheartedly. But I'm a big fan of eating my veggies, too. And an education in nutrition education had taught me that whole grains and legumes are some of the most nutrient-dense foods available.

For some reason, I was intrigued enough to dig deeper. I read *The Paleo Solution* by Robb Wolf, and everything pretty much clicked. In particular, I found some clarity on my blood sugar issues. I realized that grains weren't doing anything good for my blood sugar, so I cut them out of my diet. (Side note: in spite of of my many years of cheffery, cooking rice has always been my Achilles heel, so I considered this a win.) I've never been a fan of beans, so cutting them out wasn't all that heartbreaking either; I hardly ate them, anyway. The changes I made were subtle compared to many. With the exception of my college years, when I lived on instant noodle soups, Hamburger Helper, and beer, I have always eaten very little in the way of processed foods. My parents were hippies, after all. We didn't have store-bought salad dressing or TV dinners in the house, and our "sweet" cereal was Kix. I was given an incredibly healthy start, and my eating habits (with the exception of some dark times, such as college and several years of vegetarianism) have always been pretty good.

I'm still a chef first, and I probably will never be religious about my diet (with the exception of being gluten-free, which is not a choice). I eat some dairy. I eat rice when I go out for sushi or Thai food and snack on gluten-free crostini when I'm catering a party, and I will never, ever give up organic popcorn with good butter and sea salt. I sometimes eat too many grain-free baked goods and then decide to do a twenty-one day sugar detox to give myself a good reset. But being mostly Paleo works for me. I don't believe that there is a one-size-fits-all diet, and I encourage everyone to find what works for their own bodies and health. Start with eating real, unprocessed, nutrient-dense food, and you're on your way.

What's changed since I went mostly Paleo?

Well, pretty much everything. My health has completely turned around. If I miss a meal, the people around me don't fear for their lives. I don't feel exhausted all the time. The constant brain fog and headaches have vanished. I rarely get a cold, and when I do, I'm able to fight it off in a short amount of time. I feel good. And with the enormous list of foods that fit into this way of eating, I don't feel deprived at all.

In fact, eliminating certain foods has given me just enough of a challenge to let me really excel. I was never a great "normal" baker, but I have had incredible success with the grain-free recipes I've created.

That's probably because if I want pizza, I want *pizza*. Not the flavors of pizza in a bowl—real pizza. On my birthday, I want the chocolate cake that I remember from my childhood backyard birthday parties. And once in a while, I want warm cookies fresh out of the oven.

There is an undeniable need to satisfy that part of eating that is more than sustenance: the part that is the experience, the memory. The need to satisfy, that is what keeps me in the kitchen until I get it right.

This book, along with my catering company and blog, are realizations of that need. I know that I'm not the only one who craves the food they remember eating with their families many years ago. I'm guessing that if you're holding this book, you find joy in sharing a festive spread with good friends. To me, that's what good food is all about. I hope that the pages that follow encourage you to play with your food, go outside of your comfort zone a little bit, experiment with new flavors, and cook more food from scratch for your friends and family.

Cheers,
Simone Miller

the yes, no, and maybe lists

Depending on where you are at this moment with your diet, the following lists might either look like the best or worst news you've heard all day, or possibly somewhere in between. Wherever you're at, don't let them overwhelm you! Use these lists as a guide to help get you to stay on track and eat better. Incorporate some of the good and great stuff, and phase out the items on the "no" list at your own pace.

The good stuff

Pasture-raised or wild meats. These include beef, pork, lamb, rabbit, goat, venison, elk, and boar. Wild game is even more desirable for the latter three, but often less available.

Pasture-raised eggs. This makes a huge difference in the nutritional value of eggs, especially the yolk!

Organic free-range chicken, pastured is best.

Wild seafood and shellfish. Check seafoodwatch.org to make sure you're purchasing sustainable seafood.

Vegetables, preferably organic. Eat in-season when possible and shoot for a wide variety.

Fruits, preferably in-season and organic. Eat fruit in moderation, not as a substitute for vegetables.

Nuts, in moderation

Herbs, spices, and clean condiments. Homemade condiments are best; otherwise, read the labels.

Healthy fats. These include avocado, coconut oil, olive oil, ghee, sustainably harvested palm shortening, and animal fats such as tallow, duck fat, and lard.

The great stuff

Fermented foods

Bone broth

Organ meats

Small, oily fish, such as sardines

The gray areas

Natural sweeteners. It's tough to justify sweeteners of any kind as strictly Paleo. They're not. But since we're still human and enjoy sweet treats from time to time, there are sweeteners that are more Paleo-friendly than others. They tend to be lower glycemic and less processed than what is typically used in baked goods and sweets. I use coconut sugar (sometimes called coconut palm sugar), raw honey, and grade B maple syrup in my baked goods recipes, and sometimes in savory ones when a bit of sweet balance is called for. In moderation, I feel that these ingredients are good choices. For people who are trying to break their sugar addictions, I recommend avoiding recipes that contain any sweetener until you have that under control. The 21-Day Sugar Detox, developed by Diane Sanfilippo, is a great program to kick your carb and sugar cravings to the curb and develop better eating habits. See the21daysugardetox.com for more information.

Dairy. Technically, dairy is not Paleo, although many Paleo authorities and recipe sites include grass-fed butter and ghee as part of their Paleo template. I recommend doing an elimination diet to determine if dairy is something you tolerate or not. If it is, and you choose to consume it, I recommend raw, full-fat milk and cheeses, from pastured, organic sources when possible.

This book contains recipes that use butter as a cooking fat, as well as a small handful of recipes with full-fat dairy or cheese. In almost all cases, there is a dairy-free option listed within the recipe. If there is not, it's because there simply isn't a good alternative without losing the integrity of the recipe. I kept these recipes to a minimum, so if you avoid dairy altogether, you will still get great use out of this book.

Alcohol. Alcohol is not Paleo. Anyone who is trying to restore their health should certainly steer clear of it. However, it is a personal choice that people of legal drinking age get to make for themselves. I enjoy an adult beverage from time to time, and I don't feel like it inhibits my overall health.

There are a few recipes in this book that have wine as an ingredient. When a recipe is just as good with an alternative, I offer it, but if not, it's best to skip that one if you choose to avoid cooking with wine altogether. Again, these recipes are kept to a minimum.

White potatoes. In my opinion, the humble potato gets left off of most Paleo eating guides somewhat arbitrarily. While it's not exactly nutrient-dense, there isn't necessarily anything "not Paleo" about them. They are higher carb and higher glycemic than other tubers, so they're not a great choice for someone who is trying to lose weight or manage their blood sugar. If that's not the case for you, I don't see an issue with including them in your rotation.

The no list

Grains, especially gluten-containing grains, such as wheat, rye, and barley, but also rice, millet, quinoa, oats, teff, and corn. Although we are constantly being told that whole grains are an important part of a healthy diet, we're not getting the whole story. Grains contain powerful antinutrients, which make them difficult to digest. They also have inflammatory properties, so they are best avoided. Some people find that they tolerate white rice just fine and include it in their Paleo template. Again, it's a great idea to find what works best for you.

Legumes. You know the old song, "Beans! Beans! They're good for your heart! The more you eat, the more you fart!" But are they really good for your heart? Is farting actually heart-healthy? I am not a heart specialist, but I'm going to say no. Having excessive gas is a sign that your digestive system is having a tough time.

Industrial seed oils, "vegetable" oils such as canola, soybean, and corn

Sugar, including (I'd say especially) artificial sweeteners

Processed foods. Food without labels is best, such as fresh meats and veggies. If your food has an ingredients label, read it! If the list is longer than you have patience for reading, it's best to put it back on the shelf.

Make it work for you

As I mentioned previously, everyone does this Paleo thing differently. Some people swear off grains and legumes and dairy and never touch the stuff again. Some people need to do that to heal. I will be the first person to acknowledge that changing the way you eat is a big deal. Go with what works for you and your health goals. Tweak as necessary. And this is a biggie: DON'T STRESS. If you are tearing your hair out, afraid to leave the house for fear of starving, or on the verge of tears at the thought of grocery shopping, you're not making yourself any healthier. Trust me.

how to source the good stuff

When you think like a chef, eating Paleo is actually not that much of a stretch. No matter what their influence and style, the most important thing to all good chefs is starting with high-quality ingredients. That's what Paleo is about, too. Just about any chef would be thrilled to get a basket of Paleo-compliant ingredients and be asked to make a meal out of it.

But how do you source the good stuff? Depending on where you live, this will likely vary. As in the other areas of improving your lifestyle, I encourage you to do the best you can, and don't let perfect get in the way of good!

Here in San Francisco, where I live, I consider myself very fortunate to be in an area of food abundance, with farms and ranches within easy driving distance. I have been to the ranch I get my meat from and have even hosted a dinner there. It's exactly what you'd picture the ideal environment to be: rolling hills of seemingly endless pasture dotted with cows and sheep. The only pressure put on the chickens to lay eggs comes in the form of a toddler giving them an occasional squeeze. Fallon Hills Ranch is a fifth-generation, three-hundred-acre ranch. They raise sheep, cows, and pigs for meat, and chickens for eggs. Their beef is grass-fed and -finished, and their chickens are pastured, meaning they have access to the bugs and grubs that are in their natural diet.

Besides growing or raising food yourself, visiting the farms and ranches that produce the food you consume is the best possible sourcing scenario. You will see farming practices firsthand and feel assured that you know your food source. The next best option is to shop at farmers markets, where you can speak directly with farmers and ranchers. Don't be afraid to ask questions. If farmers are proud of how they do their jobs, they'll want to tell you about it. If they don't want to offer up any information about their practices, that's a good signal for you to keep walking.

If you're talking to a meat vendor, ask what their animals are fed, what kind of living environment they have, and if they're ever given antibiotics. Keep in mind that there's a big difference between giving a cow antibiotics on a regular basis for its whole life, as is typically done in factory-farming practices, and giving a cow a dose of antibiotics to treat an illness. Most sustainably minded farmers will tell you that if an animal has access to fresh air and pasture or foraging areas, wholesome supplementary feed, and minimal stress, antibiotics are unnecessary, except on rare occasions when the animal falls ill.

When speaking with a vegetable farmer, talk to them about how they grow their veggies; there are many growers that aren't certified organic but still grow everything organically. You can ask them what kind of pest control they use, what kind of fertilizer they use, and if they use GMO seeds.

Kevin, Erika, Clare, and Francis make up the fifth and sixth generations of Fallon Hills Ranch in Northern California.

If large, conventional supermarkets are your only option, look for local meat and produce. They may have some. You'll be more likely to find local produce if you eat what is in season. You can find seasonal produce charts at localfoods.about.com. If your budget doesn't allow you to purchase everything organic, consult the Environmental Working Group's Dirty Dozen/Clean Fifteen lists. They list the fruits and vegetables that have the highest and lowest pesticide residue, so that you can make an informed decision about how much to spend on organic produce.

If you don't have a local option for grass-fed meats, a great source is US Wellness Meats, which ships to anywhere in the United States.

For those of you lucky enough to live near family-owned farms and ranches, however, I urge you to support them by buying food directly from them, if you are able. Farmers and ranchers that do it the right way—sustainably, with the well-being of the land and animals in mind—don't have nearly the profit margins of their factory farm counterparts. It's extremely important that they stay in business, not only for our own health, but for the environment's as well.

how to stock your pantry and get equipped

When you're ready start cooking, the last thing you want to do is reach for an ingredient or tool you need and find you don't have it. This section is intended to get you well stocked with the basic ingredients and tools.

Stocking your pantry

Purge first

If you want to try to introduce more real foods into your diet, a good place to start is getting rid of the foods that aren't serving you. Read the labels of any cans, boxes, and bottles in your fridge and pantry. Are the ingredients things you could find in the store? Or do they sound like names of chemicals and artificially made frankenfoods? Donate any items you're willing to part with to a food pantry and head to the store. While the Paleo way of eating is based on unprocessed whole foods such as meats and veggies, there are plenty of pantry items to elevate your meals.

Pantry and fridge staples

Almond flour, finely ground. I like Honeyville and Wellness Bee brands, which are available online. Most store-bought almond flours or meals aren't fine enough and won't work as well in the recipes in this book. If you purchase more than you'll use within a month or so, I recommend storing it in your fridge or freezer.

Almond butter

Arrowroot powder. A key element in my grain-free flour blend, and also great for thickening soups and sauces. Arrowroot can almost always be used interchangeably with tapioca starch.

Butter, unsalted, preferably grass-fed (if you tolerate dairy)

Capers. Packed in salt for the best flavor, but brined is fine, too.

Chipotle peppers or paste. Canned chipotle peppers add a spicy smokiness like nothing else can. Just be sure to check the ingredients, as many use wheat flour as a thickening agent. A great alternative is the chipotle paste from Chipotle People (chipotlepeople.com).

Cocoa powder, either good-quality fair trade cocoa powder or raw cacao

Coconut aminos. An excellent replacement for soy sauce and tamari.

Coconut flour. One of three flours in my special grain-free baking blend. Coconut flour is extremely absorbent and, when used alone, requires lots of eggs and moisture to balance it out. Used as part of a blend, it provides great balance to the almond flour and arrowroot powder.

Coconut milk, full-fat, canned. Look for BPA-free cans.

Curry paste (red, green, and/or yellow). Make sure the ingredients are clean; I like Mae Ploy and Thai Kitchen brands because they have clean ingredients and no additives.

Dijon mustard. Check the ingredients to make sure it's gluten-free. Some contain malt vinegar and beer for flavoring. Many also contain sugar, which you'll want to avoid if you're on a sugar detox of any kind.

Duck fat. An excellent cooking fat, rich and somewhat neutral in flavor. Store in the fridge.

Extra virgin coconut oil

Fish sauce. Red Boat brand is highly recommended because it only contains fish and salt—unlike most brands, it doesn't have any added sugar.

Extra virgin olive oil. Best used in nonheat applications.

Gelatin. Look for gelatin from grass-fed cows. I like the brands Great Lakes and Vital Proteins.

Ghee. Clarifying butter removes the lactose, making it a healthier choice for those who can't tolerate dairy. It also results in a fat that, unlike butter, has a high smoke point, making it a great choice for higher-heat cooking.

Jarred tomatoes (crushed, diced). Look for brands that contain only tomatoes and salt. Buying tomatoes in glass jars is best; if you buy canned tomatoes, make sure the cans are BPA-free.

Kombu. This variety of seaweed adds a great depth of flavor, umami, and calcium to broths and soups.

Lard. If you can find lard that is rendered from properly raised pigs, it's a great choice for cooking and even baking. Store in the fridge.

Light olive oil. Somewhat controversial in the Paleosphere, this is technically more processed than we like our oils to be, but it's extremely versatile as a neutral-flavored oil.

Nuts and seeds: almonds, pecans, walnuts, macadamia nuts, pistachios, pine nuts, cashews, sunflower seeds, pumpkin seeds

Palm shortening. Please make sure to purchase a brand that is sustainably sourced, such as Tropical Traditions.

Sesame seeds, black and/or white

Toasted sesame oil

Tahini

Tapioca starch. Great for grain-free baking and for thickening sauces. Tapioca starch can almost always be used interchangeably with arrowroot.

Tomato paste

Vanilla extract or vanilla bean paste

Vinegars: red wine, white wine, balsamic, apple cider, champagne. Avoid malt vinegar; it is made from barley and isn't distilled, as others are, and so contains gluten.

Dried herbs and spices

Black pepper, freshly ground yields the best flavor

Smoked paprika

Cumin, ground

Coriander, ground

Cayenne pepper

Oregano leaves

Chipotle powder

Chile powder, ancho (not to be confused with chili powder, which is a blend of several spices)

Cinnamon, ground and stick

Cardamom, pods and ground

Ground ginger

Dry mustard

Garlic powder

Garam masala

Saffron

Sumac

Ground turmeric

Salt is born of the purest of parents: the sun and the sea.
~ Pythagoras

Salt. The recipes in this book were created using finely ground sea salt, unless otherwise noted. If you are using a different kind of salt, you may need to adjust the measurement a bit. To use kosher or table salt in place of sea salt, use ¾ teaspoon for each teaspoon as instructed. Please don't fear the salt. It's necessary in every recipe, and there is no replacement for it.

Ingredient shortcuts

It's true that eating within a Paleo template means that you'll probably be cooking most of your food from scratch. There isn't really a way around that. But I'd be lying if I said I took this 100-percent literally. As someone who often needs to make a lot of food in a short amount of time, I've found some shortcuts that make my life easier. An important note: Getting fresh seasonal produce from your local farmers market or a CSA is always the best choice, hands down. However, if you have limited time or simply get frustrated and bored in the kitchen, cut yourself some slack and do what you've got to do. Anyone making the transition to a real-foods way of life deserves some credit for making a fantastic decision for their health.

Jarred tomatoes. Make sure that the only ingredients are tomatoes and maybe some herbs or salt. If you have a garden and are able to can your own, even better. I don't have a vegetable garden myself, for moral reasons. Those poor plants wouldn't stand a chance.

Peeled garlic and shallots. This is a tough one. Please do not buy dried-up shallots or garlic that is turning brown or sprouting in a plastic container a shelf just because they're already peeled. We still want to focus on quality. If you're shopping in a store that goes through a lot of the stuff and it looks super fresh, go for it. Of course, if you happen to find it meditative to peel garlic and shallots and aren't pressed for time, by all means, continue buying it intact. But if time is of the essence and it's all you can do to get in the kitchen and cook dinner for your family, don't sweat getting a little help here.

Roasted bell peppers. Roasting peppers on a gas flame or under the broiler isn't horribly difficult. Again, if you love doing this, please do. It will make your house smell smoky in a good way and is a fun little project. But if you're looking for an easy way to add a smoky depth to a dish, having a jar of roasted peppers on hand is an effortless way of doing so.

Steamed beets. Here's the thing: Beets are not a difficult thing to roast or steam. There is a recipe for them in this book, in fact. However, I am absolutely guilty of buying beautiful bunches of beets at the farmers market and letting them sit night after night, always selecting a different side dish until there are no other ones to choose. I can't say exactly why, but I'm guessing that maybe I'm not the only one who does this. If you are 99-percent more likely to consume beets if you purchase them ready to eat, it's worth it. But keep in mind I'm talking about the ones in the produce aisle, still perishable and without strange ingredients added, not the canned variety.

Getting equipped

Choosing a knife

The most important tool in your kitchen arsenal is a knife. Get a good sharp one, or three. Or twelve. You don't necessarily need to sell your car to buy a good set of knives, but there are some things you want to consider when you do purchase them.

Full tang. This means that the knife blade and handle are forged from one solid piece of metal—the handle hasn't been attached to the blade. This raises the price of the knife a bit, but it's worth it. It makes the knife much stronger and likely to last a lot longer.

Weight. Go to a store with a large selection. Hold the knives in your hand to see how they feel. This is important! You are going to be using the knife a lot; it needs to feel like a good fit for you. If it feels light and cheap, it probably is. But if it feels burdensome to hold, that's not good either. Don't feel bad about asking to see lots of knives before making a decision.

Price. Do some research before you head to a store so you know what to expect and have an idea of what you can afford. You can easily spend thousands of dollars on good knives, but it is also completely possible to get a great set for a reasonable price. Many knife companies offer starter sets that include two to three knives, a sharpening steel, kitchen shears, and a knife block. This is a great starting point, and you can slowly build your collection from there.

How many? This is somewhat up to you. A good knife collection is something that you can build over the years, once you discover which kinds you like to use. To start your collection, I recommend you have:

- **A chef's knife.** Eight inches is a good middle-of-the-road size, but go with what feels best for you. I have a 9-inch and a 7-inch and use them both all the time.

- **A santoku knife.** Also called a Japanese vegetable knife, this is extremely versatile and useful for everything from mincing shallots to chopping carrots to removing the stones from avocados.

- **A carving knife.** For slicing steaks, roasts, and seared fish dishes cleanly and evenly.

- **A paring knife.** For small jobs such as hulling strawberries and eyeing potatoes, and for making small, precise cuts.

- **A utility knife.** For general small tasks— great for tomatoes, peeling and cutting citrus, and much more.

After spending some money on a good knife, you'll want to take care of it properly. Here are some basics on knife care:

- Always wash and dry knives by hand after using them.

- Have an appropriate knife sharpener for the types of knives you have, and get your knives professionally sharpened at least twice a year. Most kitchen stores offer knife sharpening, but if you have quality Japanese knives, such as Shun, I recommend taking them to a shop that sharpens them by hand (unless you are skilled at sharpening them yourself with a whetstone).

Having the right tools

When I go to someone's home to cater a party, I assume that they have nothing in their kitchen for me to use and bring all the tools I could possibly need. I'm always glad that I plan this way, because a lot of people are missing essentials I just can't live without. This is completely fine for someone who doesn't do much cooking, but if you're spending a lot of time in the kitchen, you'll have a much better experience if you have the right tools.

Wooden spoons, round and flat-edged. For stirring and sautéeing.

Tongs. Once I put my knife down, these become the extension of my hand. They're indispensable for flipping and moving around food while cooking. Get some good sturdy ones that lock closed.

Spatulas. I like having both metal and silicone spatulas for flipping, stirring, and sautéeing.

Ladles. A few different sizes are essential for serving and transferring soups and stews. Also, they make skimming the fat from broths and sauces effortless: Pour into a wide-mouth glass jar and plunge in a small ladle to remove the fat that rises to the top.

Julienne peeler and/or **spiral slicer** (aka Spiralizer, the most popular brand of spiral slicer). Allows you to make ribbons and noodles out of just about anything. Essential for making zucchini noodles.

Brushes. For basting meats and applying egg wash to pie crusts.

Rasp grater (aka Microplane). For zesting citrus and grating ginger and garlic. This tool is always either in the sink or on the drain board in my kitchen; I use it almost daily.

Blender. Essential for making smooth sauces, smoothies, and soups. I recommend Blendtec.

Food processor. The grater attachment will yield perfect cauliflower rice, and the chopper blade will speed up your prep time when you're mincing or pureeing raw veggies. I recommend Quisinart.

Disher (ice cream scoop with a lever). They come in different sizes; I get the most use out of my 1.5-ounce and 2-ounce sizes.

Handheld immersion blender. Lets you puree soups and sauces without transferring them to a blender. Also essential for making effortless mayonnaise and vinaigrettes.

Assorted mixing bowls and prep bowls

Measuring spoons

Measuring cups, dry and liquid

Kitchen scale

Cookware and bakeware

- Small cast iron and/or stainless steel sauté pan
- Stainless steel saucepans in a variety of sizes
- Tempered glass baking dishes (I use 8-inch-square and 9-by-13-inch dishes most)
- Large stainless steel stockpot (8- to 10-quart)
- Cast iron Dutch oven
- Large cast iron and/or stainless steel skillet (10-inch)
- Pressure cooker (optional, but great for speeding up broth cooking time)
- Rimmed baking sheets (aka sheet pans)
- Large roasting pan
- 12-cup muffin tin
- 7-inch loaf pan
- 9-inch tart pan
- 9-inch springform pans (2)

Other useful items

- Aluminum foil
- Glass jars and other storage containers
- Kitchen towels (I find that "more than you think you'll need" is about the right amount!)
- Paper towels
- Parchment muffin liners
- Parchment paper
- Plastic wrap

how to cook like a pro

Picking up some good kitchen habits (like mise en place), getting a solid handle on some basic cooking techniques (and the lingo for them; see the glossary on page 274), and learning a basic set of knife cuts will set you on the path to cooking like a pro.

Basic techniques

Before you begin

Start with a solid surface. Place a damp cloth or nonslip drawer liner under your cutting board to keep it from moving. Combating a moving cutting board while yielding a sharp knife isn't a good start. Plastic cutting boards that roll up are not safe and don't do anything good for your knife skills. A large wooden or bamboo board is a must.

How to: Hold a knife

Rest the knife on the inside of your index finger, where the blade meets the handle. It should more or less balance there.

Place your thumb on the other side of the blade.

Allow your grip on the knife to be partially on the top of the blade. This will give you more control.

Please don't do this.

And don't death-grip the handle.

inside eggrolls
mexican beef & zucch
cheesy chicken & spag. squash

How to: Keep all of your fingers

Position the hand that is not holding the knife in a C shape, so that the tips of your fingers are pointing down towards the cutting board and at a slight angle away from the knife blade. In kitchen-speak, this is called "the claw." Gripping the food this way will result in better control and lessen the chances of fingernails (or worse, fingers) in your meal.

How to: Julienne a carrot
(or any other ingredient that doesn't start off rectangular)

Cut to the length that you want your matchsticks to be.

Slice off one of the rounded sides so you have a flat surface.

Turn the carrot flat side down on your board and make thin, lengthwise cuts.

Make sure you use "the claw" to maintain control of the carrot.

Stack up the slices.

And slice them again, as thin as you did in Step 3.

How to: Core, julienne, mince, and dice a bell pepper

1

Cut off the top and bottom of the pepper. You can chop them up for salad or soup, or just snack on them.

2

Turn the pepper on its side. Hold your hand on the top of the pepper and, where it is closest to the cutting board, make an incision with your knife parallel to the cutting board.

3

Keeping your knife horizontal to the cutting board, cut into the pepper, moving around the core and rolling the pepper as you go with your top hand.

4

Keep rolling.

5

And rolling.

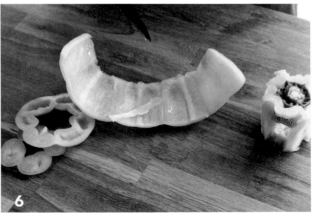

6

Until the core comes loose and you're left with the perfectly deconstructed pepper!

7

Now you have a somewhat rectangular shape to work with. With a nice, flat piece of pepper, it's easy to . . .

8

Julienne

9

Mince

10

Cut into strips

11

Or dice . . .

12

Small, medium, or large

How to: Dice or mince an onion

1

Slice off the papery end of the onion.

2

Slice it in half lengthwise.

3

Peel.

4

Place it cut side down and slice lengthwise, from the core down.

5

Turn the onion 90 degrees and slice across your lengthwise cuts in the same thickness.

6

Keep slicing until you get to the core end.

How to: Supreme an orange or create orange wheels

1

Slice off the top and bottom of the orange with a utility knife, paring knife, or small chef's knife.

2

Stand the orange up and cut between the peel and the flesh at an angle, following the contour of the orange. Remove as little flesh as possible while making sure to get all of the pith

3

Continue to work your way around the orange, cutting off the peel in a curved motion.

4

Once the orange is peeled, you can cut it crosswise or in thick or thin circles, or you can supreme it, as follows.

5

Hold the orange in your hand and carefully cut along one side of the segment, getting as close to the membrane as possible.

6

Repeat on the other side of the segment, so you release the segment from the membrane. Collect the segments in small bowl.

7

Repeat with the remaining segments until you're left with just the center of the orange and the membranes. (You can throw what's left in a smoothie, or squeeze the juice out of it to use in a recipe.)

How to: Chiffonade herbs

Stack.

Roll.

Slice.

How to: Cut up a whole chicken

Check the inside of the chicken for a bag containing the innards. Rinse the chicken and pat dry with paper towels. Place on a sturdy cutting board.

Cut off any loose skin or fat around the neck and cavity.

Locate the fat line between the leg and the body.

Cut along the fat line, following the contour of the side of the body.

Cut all the way through, doing your best to cut between the joints.

Repeat on the other side.

Turn the chicken on its side and lift it up by its wing. Allowing the weight of the chicken to help you, cut off the wing where it attaches to the breast. Repeat on the other side.

With the breast facing up, insert your knife between the sides of the breast and the back. With a sawing motion, cut from the cavity to the neck, going through the side rib bones.

9

Continue to cut all the way up to the top of the breast.

10

Pull the backbone and the breast away from each other to break the body apart.

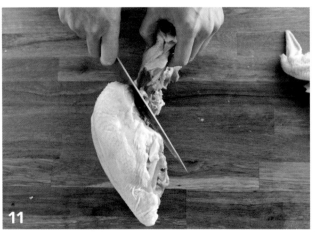

11

Cut through the small amount of bone and cartilage that is still attached.

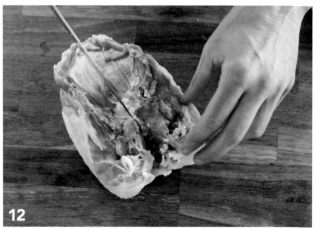

12

Once you're left with the breast, flip it skin side down and cut into the middle of the breastbone, just enough to perforate it. This will make it easier to break the bone.

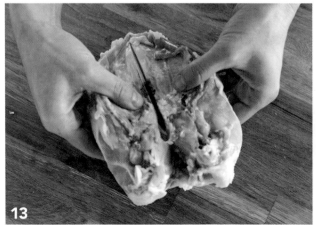

13

Bend the breast backwards to break the bone.

14

Place it skin side up on the board and press down, in the middle of the breast. Cut straight down the middle of the breast, separating it into halves.

15

Cut the wing tips off the wings by slicing between the joints.

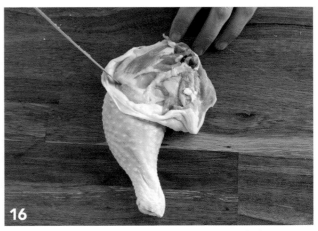

16

To separate the leg from the thigh (optional), locate the fat line that runs between the thigh and the leg.

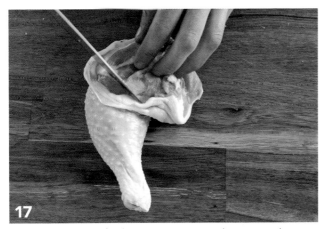

17

Cut through the fat line, trying to get between the joints as much as possible. Repeat on the other leg.

And there you have it! A whole chicken, all cut up and organized neatly. You can cut the breast in half crosswise to yield smaller pieces, but I recommend doing so after cooking if you plan on cooking the whole chicken at once. White meat cooks faster than dark, so it's a good thing that the breast pieces are larger than the dark meat pieces.

Reserve the backbone and wing tips for stock. Save them in a plastic bag in the freezer if not using right away, or throw them straight into a small stockpot and make a quick batch while you cook your chicken.

18

How to: Cook en papillote

While there is only one recipe in this book that uses this method, my hope is that you'll be inspired to create your own en papillote recipes. The premise is simple: Foods are baked in a parchment envelope that traps the aromatic steam and infuses lots of flavor into the dish. You can cook just about anything this way. Experiment with different types of fish and seafood, boneless chicken, starchy vegetables, and even fruits (as a great low-glycemic dessert option).

1

Gather all of the ingredients you plan on cooking in your parchment envelope.

2

Set out a large sheet of parchment paper

3

Fold it in half, making a sharp crease

4

Starting on the folded side, begin to cut a large heart shape.

5

Continue to cut a heart in the paper

6

Until you get to the bottom point.

7 Open the parchment to reveal the heart shape you cut

8 Place the main ingredients on one side of the heart.

9 Add butter or some kind of fat.

10 And herbs, seasonings, and a small amount of liquid.

11

12

Steps 11 to 12: Fold the empty half of the heart over the ingredients.

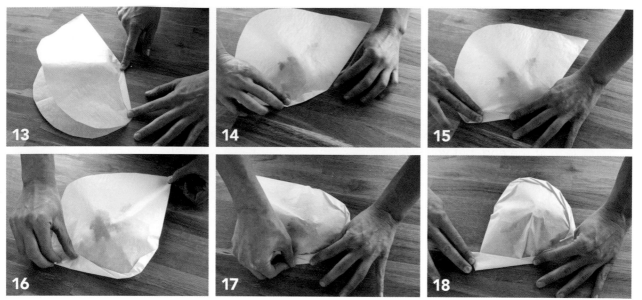

Steps 13 to 18: Beginning with the inside edge of the heart, make a fold of about an inch long. Make a second fold, starting from about half way in from the first one, so that they overlap and seal the parchment. Continue doing this until you get to the bottom point of the heart.

Steps 19 to 20: Once you get to the bottom point, grab the remaining parchment and twist several times in the same direction you were making your folds.

Set up your mise en place

After you've minced, chopped, or julienned your ingredients, it's helpful to organize them so they're in easy reach and ready to use as you're cooking. Mise en place, literally "put in place," is chef-speak for doing just that. Set up your kitchen as if you're about to do a cooking demo: Wash and prep herbs, measure spices, dice vegetables, and season meats. You might wind up with a few more small bowls to clean at the end, but you will be much more efficient and will likely enjoy cooking a whole lot more!

How to: Build flavor

We're starting with great ingredients, and that means that it often takes less coaxing and fussing to get their best flavor to come through. To me, cooking is all about giving ingredients just the right treatment to get them to sing and be balanced within the recipe, and to create a dish that is greater than the sum of its parts.

The recipes in this book are somewhat specific about the order and technique in which the steps should be done. There is a good reason for this. On some occasions, mixing all of the ingredients together in one step yields a perfect result (such as adding ingredients to mayonnaise to make aioli). However, many recipes require a bit more finesse. The best way to describe this is with an example: cauliflower soup. You could, very easily, heat up some broth; add the raw cauliflower, onions, and salt; cook until soft; and puree. You would, undoubtedly, have cauliflower soup. But would it be delicious cauliflower soup? Not really. Roasting the cauliflower and the onions in some fat first completely changes the flavor of this soup. Adding a bit of broth to the roasting pan to deglaze the fond that formed while roasting elevates the flavor even further. And simmering the roasted veggies in the broth marries all the flavors together. It might not be all that groundbreaking, but it makes the difference between decent food and excellent food.

The order in which ingredients are added to the pan is intentional as well. Onions take longer to cook than peppers, which take longer to cook than garlic. While I could combine three steps into one to make a recipe shorter, I don't do that, because the end result will suffer. Cooking garlic for ten minutes with sliced onions will ensure overcooked or burned garlic. My intention with this book is to help you learn cooking techniques that will help you to become a better cook, beyond following recipes. Once you learn the foundations, you'll find that creating excellent food with quality ingredients is easier than you may have thought.

how to use this book

I organized this book as if I were spending the day in the kitchen. First you will find sauces, condiments, and basic recipes. Think of this chapter as the foundation for your kitchen arsenal. Some of these sauces are used in recipes later on, while others are there to help you take your cooking to the next level.

Next, you will find recipes that take you from breakfast to dinner, including appetizers, soups and salads, and breads and wraps. My intention is that as you cook your way through this book, you will never feel as if anything is missing from your diet—Paleo or not. As a bonus, I hope you find that the food coming out of your kitchen is the best it's ever been.

At the end of the book is a menus section, where I offer cohesive menus to help inspire you to invite friends and family over to celebrate good food and good health.

Recipe breakdown

When trying a new recipe, always read the entire recipe before starting to gather your ingredients. It takes thirty seconds, and you will save way more time than that if you go into the recipe with an understanding of what you'll be doing.

Here, quickly, is how the recipes in this book are broken down.

---

prep time: 5 minutes | **cook time:** 10 to 15 minutes | **serves:** 4 / **makes:** 1 cup

---

Prep time: Time needed to get a recipe ready to cook, including marinating. Does not include preparing an additional recipe that is part of the one in question (for example, making tortillas for fajitas).

Cook time: Actual cooking time, including both active and inactive time, such as the time required to allow a roast to sit before carving.

Serves/makes: Based on four adults or hungry kids. Most recipes in the book are written for four. In the case of appetizers and small bites, the portions are intended to be smaller and feed more people. In the case of sauces or condiments, the recipe states how much it makes (1 quart, for instance) rather than how many it serves.

---

3 tablespoons lemon juice oil, divided *

1 tablespoon butter, ghee, or preferred cooking fat **

¼ cup chopped fresh parsley (about 1 small bunch) ***

---

*   When you see "divided" in an ingredients list, it means that the ingredient in question will be used in more than one place in a recipe. It's a heads-up, essentially, not to throw it all in the first time you come across the ingredient in the instructions.

** I often offer options for cooking fats and name first the one I recommend most highly for the recipe. This is based mostly on the flavor of each specific recipe, but often any fat will work and you can feel free to use whichever you'd like. I sometimes use light olive oil for cooking, which I know is frowned upon in the Paleo community because it's not a stable cooking fat. While I agree, I still do use it sparingly for frying or sautéing when I am in need of a neutral-tasting oil.

***The primary measurement corresponds to the amount after it's stemmed and chopped. The amount in parentheses is there to give you an idea of what you'll need to start with.

About the measurements

Onions come in all sizes. If a recipe calls for "1 onion," which do you choose? The recipes in this book present measurements of most vegetables, both in size of the original vegetable and the volume in produces when prepped. This doesn't mean that you have to measure incessantly each time you cook, but it will give you a good idea of what I had in mind when I wrote the recipe. If you're wondering why I'm a bit obsessed with onion sizes: Imagine you're following a recipe for a simple tomato salsa that calls for "1 onion." The recipe writer probably had a tiny onion in mind when writing the recipe, but you don't know that and go with the jumbo onion. You could lose friends that way, especially when raw onion is involved.

tiny: 3 ounces / ½ cup diced

small: 6 ounces / 1½ cups diced

medium: 9 ounces / 2 cups diced

large: 14 ounces / 2¾ cups diced

jumbo: 1¼ pounds / 4 cups diced

About the ingredients photos

Each recipe in this book has a photograph of the ingredients used in the recipe, organized neatly. These photos are meant to be both helpful and beautiful. They are not intended to take the place of the written ingredients list but rather to give you a visual of the ingredients you'll be gathering to make the dish. I love these shots because they often highlight just how few ingredients are needed to create an incredible dish. Think of the ingredients photo as the "before" and the plated photo as the "after." Ingredients photos do not include seasoning salt or pepper (which are in nearly every dish) or the fat used for cooking the dish. The exception to this is when salt is more than a flavor enhancer in the recipe—for example, in Perfect Roast Chicken (page 158) or Guacamole (page 48), the salt is more of a technique than simply an ingredient.

SAUCES, CONDIMENTS, AND BASICS

guacamole

prep time: **20 minutes** | makes: **about 1 cup**

Rejoice, guacamole lovers! Gone are the days of ugly brown guacamole. A quick salt water soak is the secret to keeping guacamole a beautiful bright green. While we're on the subject of green, it's the only color you'll see in this recipe. Before you shout "Blasphemy!" and start chopping red onions and tomatoes, try my version. It might just be your new favorite.

¼ cup finely ground sea salt

½ cup hot water plus 1½ cups cold water

3 avocados, peeled, halved, and pitted

1 jalapeño pepper, minced (membrane and seeds removed for mild guacamole)

2 tablespoons minced fresh cilantro

3 scallions, thinly sliced

2 tablespoons lime juice

01 Combine the salt and the ½ cup of hot water in a large bowl and stir to dissolve the salt. Then stir in the 1½ cups of cold water.

02 Place the peeled avocado halves in the salt water and let them soak for 15 minutes.

03 After their salt soak, remove the avocados from the bowl and rinse it out to make sure there's no excess salt at the bottom.

04 Return the avocados to the bowl and add the jalapeño, cilantro, scallions, and lime juice.

05 Mash with a whisk until well incorporated, making it as creamy or chunky as you'd like.

avocado mousse

prep time: **20 minutes** | makes: **about 1 cup**

Avocados take on a sublimely creamy texture when blended until smooth. Giving them a soak in salt water will keep the mousse green—no need to worry about the ugly brown avocado syndrome. Serve this as a creamy alternative to guacamole or with Mango-Chile Ceviche (page 102), or dollop it on Onion Eggs (page 76).

¼ cup finely ground sea salt

½ cup hot water plus 1½ cups cold water

2 firm yet ripe avocados, peeled, halved, and pitted

1 tablespoon lime juice

½ teaspoon ground coriander

1 to 2 pinches of cayenne pepper (optional)

01 Combine the salt and the ½ cup of hot water in a large bowl and stir to dissolve the salt. Then stir in the 1½ cups of cold water.

02 Drop the avocado halves in the salt water. Let sit for 15 minutes.

03 After their salt soak, remove the avocados from the salt water and give them a quick rinse. Transfer them to a food processor.

04 Add the lime juice and coriander and blend until smooth. If you want it spicy, add a pinch or two of cayenne pepper.

vinaigrettes

Once you discover how easy it is to make your own vinaigrettes at home, you'll wonder why you ever bothered with the store-bought variety. The following three recipes will cover most of your salad needs, but you'll love how easy it is to get creative and whip up your own variations!

Drizzling in the oil will result in a good, thick, emulsified dressing, but if that sounds like more than you want to deal with after a long day, you can also put all of the ingredients in a jar with a tight-fitting lid and give it a good shake. You'll just need to shake it each time you use it, as the ingredients will separate.

basil balsamic vinaigrette

prep time: **10 minutes** | makes: **about 1 cup**

Great on: hearty green salads, roasted or grilled veggies, steak

¼ cup balsamic vinegar

1 tablespoon Dijon mustard

⅛ teaspoon finely ground sea salt

pinch of ground black pepper

½ cup extra virgin olive oil

1 tablespoon minced fresh basil

01 In a medium bowl, whisk together the vinegar, mustard, salt, and pepper.

02 Slowly drizzle in the olive oil, whisking constantly.

03 Stir in the basil.

04 Store in a glass jar in the refrigerator for up to 2 weeks.

blood orange vinaigrette

prep time: **10 minutes** | makes: **about 1 cup**

Great on: Roasted Beet and Orange Salad (page 114), seared scallops, bitter greens such as arugula and frisée

2 tablespoons white wine vinegar

¼ cup blood orange juice

2 teaspoons Dijon mustard

¼ teaspoon finely ground sea salt

⅛ teaspoon ground black pepper

½ cup extra virgin olive oil

½ teaspoon minced fresh thyme

01 In a medium bowl, whisk together the vinegar, blood orange juice, mustard, salt, and pepper.

02 Slowly drizzle in the olive oil, whisking constantly.

03 Stir in the thyme.

04 Store in a glass jar in the refrigerator for up to 2 weeks.

champagne vinaigrette

prep time: **10 minutes** | makes: **about 1 cup**

Great on: springtime salads with strawberries; lighter, milder greens such as butter lettuce; asparagus; roasted potatoes

¼ cup champagne vinegar

1 teaspoon Dijon mustard

1 teaspoon honey

½ teaspoon finely ground sea salt

¼ teaspoon ground black pepper

¾ cup extra virgin olive oil

1 tablespoon minced fresh chives

01 In a medium bowl, whisk together the vinegar, mustard, honey, salt, and pepper.

02 Slowly drizzle in the olive oil, whisking constantly.

03 Stir in the chives.

04 Store in a glass jar in the refrigerator for up to 2 weeks.

basil balsamic vinaigrette

blood orange vinaigrette

champagne vinaigrette

mayonnaise

prep time: **10 minutes** | makes: **about 1 cup**

Making homemade mayonnaise is simpler than you might think, and effortless when you use an immersion blender. Mayonnaise emulsifies best when all of the ingredients are at room temperature.

3 egg yolks

1 tablespoon apple cider vinegar

½ teaspoon finely ground sea salt

¾ cup oil (light olive oil, macadamia oil, avocado oil, or a combination), divided

2 tablespoons water

1 tablespoon lemon juice

01 Place the egg yolks and vinegar in a wide-mouthed quart-sized glass jar, or similar-sized vessel. Blend with an immersion blender for 1 minute.

02 Add the salt and blend again.

03 With the motor running, slowly drizzle in ½ cup of the oil, keeping the stream small. Incorporate the oil by moving the blender in small up-and-down circles.

04 Add the water and blend until combined.

05 Slowly drizzle in the remaining ¼ cup of oil, continuing to run the blender.

06 Blend in the lemon juice.

07 Store in a jar in the refrigerator for up to 5 days.

 Got good whisking muscles? Make this by hand with a wire whisk in a large bowl. Make sure to add the oil very slowly, and keep whisking!

dijon-herb aioli

prep time: **10 minutes** | makes: **about 1¼ cups**

Fresh herbs and tangy Dijon mustard combine to create what might just be the most versatile condiment there is. It's perfect on fish or chicken, or as a dip for vegetables.

¼ cup minced fresh chives (about 20 chives)

2 tablespoons minced fresh parsley

1 teaspoon minced fresh tarragon (1 small sprig)

1 teaspoon finely grated lemon zest

2 tablespoons Dijon mustard

¼ teaspoon finely ground sea salt

1 batch Mayonnaise (page 54)

01 Place the chives, parsley, and tarragon in a medium mixing bowl.

02 Add the lemon zest, mustard, salt, and mayonnaise.

03 Stir to combine.

04 Store in a glass jar in the refrigerator for up to 1 week.

garlic-dill aioli

prep time: **35 minutes** | makes: **about 1¼ cups**

This aioli is based on my dad's signature creamy garlic salad dressing. The earthiness of the dill is balanced out by a good kick of raw garlic. It's equal parts pungent, mellow, and peppery, and it's great with grilled fish, on roasted vegetables, or mixed into canned or cooked tuna for a quick, easy tuna salad.

2 cloves garlic, grated or minced

2 teaspoons white wine vinegar

1 batch Mayonnaise (page 54)

¼ cup minced fresh dill

1 teaspoon Dijon mustard

¼ teaspoon finely ground salt

⅛ teaspoon ground black pepper

 Variation: Add 2 tablespoons of water to the finished aioli for a creamy salad dressing.

01 Place the garlic and vinegar in a medium mixing bowl. Allow to sit for 15 to 30 minutes to allow the garlic to mellow a bit.

02 Add the mayonnaise, dill, Dijon mustard, salt, and pepper to the bowl and stir to combine.

03 Store in a glass jar in the refrigerator for up to 1 week.

rémoulade

prep time: **10 minutes, plus up to 45 minutes to roast the peppers**
| makes: **about 1¼ cups**

When I lived in upstate New York, I worked at a sweet little restaurant called Simply Red Village Bistro. On Monday nights, we strayed from the usual upscale menu and served up a southern menu, with some Cajun influence. Simply Red is where I was first introduced to rémoulade, and I have loved it ever since. Think of it as a sophisticated tarter sauce: smoky, tangy, briny, and rich. Serve it dolloped on your favorite fish cakes or as the dipping sauce for Cilantro-Lime Roasted Shrimp (page 150), or dip sweet potato fries in it.

1 bell pepper, roasted (red, orange, or yellow; see Notes)

1 tablespoon minced fresh parsley

1 tablespoon minced scallion bottoms (white part only)

1 tablespoon minced scallion tops (green part only)

1 cup Mayonnaise (page 54)

1 tablespoon Dijon mustard

1 tablespoon lemon juice

½ teaspoon paprika

¼ teaspoon chipotle powder

2 tablespoons capers, rinsed and drained

¼ teaspoon finely ground sea salt

01   Mince the roasted pepper. Combine the pepper, parsley, and scallions in a medium mixing bowl.

02   Add the mayonnaise, mustard, lemon juice, paprika, chipotle powder, capers, and salt.

03   Stir to combine.

04   Store in a glass jar in the refrigerator for up to 1 week.

NOTES

- To roast the peppers over a gas flame: Turn the burner to medium-high and place the peppers directly on the grate above the burner. Allow the peppers to blister and blacken before turning them with tongs. Keep blistering and turning them until they are blackened all the way around. Remove to a heatproof bowl and cover with plastic wrap.

- To roast the peppers in the oven: Turn the broiler to high and position an oven rack in the top tier. Place the peppers on a baking sheet and broil for 25 to 30 minutes, turning every 5 minutes or so, until they are blackened all the way around. Remove to a heat-proof bowl and cover with plastic wrap.

- Remove the peel: After the peppers have steamed in the bowl for 15 minutes, remove them and rub off the peels. While it's tempting to simply run them under water, this will remove a lot of the smoky flavor, so try to be patient and peel them without water.

stir-fry marinade and sauce

prep time: **5 minutes** | makes: **¾ cup**

Once you discover how versatile this sauce is, you'll want to always keep the ingredients on hand to whip up a batch. Use it in a stir-fry, toss it with cabbage and other julienned veggies for a quick Asian slaw, or marinate your salmon before throwing it on the grill . . . all the while wondering why you ever bought the stuff that comes in a bottle.

½ cup coconut aminos

⅓ cup orange juice (from 1 large orange; see Note)

2 teaspoons fish sauce

1 (1-inch) piece ginger, peeled and grated

2 cloves garlic, minced

2 teaspoons chili paste or Sriracha sauce

01 Place all of the ingredients in a small bowl. Stir to combine.

02 Store in a jar in the refrigerator for up to 1 week.

 Note: If you plan on making Orange-Ginger Beef Stir-Fry (page 202), use a vegetable peeler to peel off wide strips of zest (the outermost, colored part of the peel) before juicing the orange. Reserve the zest.

lemony hollandaise sauce

prep time: **5 minutes** | cook time: **5 minutes** | makes: **1½ cups**

It's entirely possible that there is simply nothing better than hollandaise sauce. It's rich, creamy, lemony, and decadent. Drizzle it on Roasted Asparagus (page 218), over any simply cooked seafood, and of course on Eggs Benedict (page 80). I love it extra lemony with just a tiny kick of cayenne, but feel free to season it to your liking.

4 egg yolks

1 to 2 tablespoons lemon juice

8 tablespoons unsalted butter, melted

½ teaspoon finely ground sea salt

dash of white or cayenne pepper

01 In a medium heatproof bowl, vigorously whisk the egg yolks with 1 tablespoon of lemon juice.

02 Place the bowl over a pot of barely simmering water.

03 Continue whisking the yolks until they are warm, but don't let them get so hot that they scramble.

04 Slowly drizzle in the melted butter while whisking constantly. Continue whisking until the mixture thickens, about 3 minutes.

05 Whisk in the salt and season to taste with additional lemon juice and white pepper or cayenne.

06 If not using right away, keep warm over the warm water with the burner off. If reheating, place in a small saucepan over low heat and add a bit of hot water to thin as needed; whisk constantly until warm, about 2 minutes.

chimichurri

prep time: **10 minutes** | makes: **about 1¼ cups**

Few condiments match the intensely bright punch of chimichurri. Most Americanized versions of this Argentinean sauce include cilantro, but the traditional recipe calls for oregano. For a quick and satisfying weeknight meal, grill up some steaks and give them a good drizzle of chimichurri.

1 bunch fresh parsley, leafy portion torn off the stems (discard stems or use for stock)

2 tablespoons fresh oregano leaves

2 cloves garlic, minced

1 tablespoon red wine vinegar

½ teaspoon red pepper flakes, plus more to taste

¼ teaspoon finely ground salt, plus more to taste

¾ cup extra virgin olive oil

01 Put all of the ingredients except the olive oil in the bowl of a food processor. Pulse a few times to coarsely chop. (For a coarser sauce, the herbs can also be chopped by hand.)

02 Add the olive oil and pulse a few times more to incorporate. It should be the consistency of a rough pesto.

03 Season to taste with additional salt and red pepper flakes, if desired.

 Bonus recipe! Mix a couple of tablespoons of chimichurri into a batch of homemade Mayonnaise (page 54) for a killer burger or grilled chicken condiment.

raita

prep time: **10 minutes** | makes: **about 1¼ cups**

I love raita so much that when I go out for Indian food, I get my main dish a little bit spicier than I can tolerate—just so I have an excuse to use lots of raita to balance out the heat. I just love the cooling combination of yogurt, cucumber, and mint. For a dairy-free version, use coconut cream; it's just as delicious. But you'll need to plan ahead: Place a can of coconut milk in the fridge overnight. Open it without shaking, and the cream should have settled on top of the water. Scoop out just the cream for this recipe. You can reserve the remaining water to add to a curry or a smoothie.

½ cup grated cucumber (¼ pound or 1 small) (see Note)

¼ cup fresh mint leaves, minced

¾ cup full-fat yogurt or coconut cream (from a can of refrigerated coconut milk)

2 tablespoons lemon juice

¼ teaspoon finely ground sea salt

pinch of ground black pepper

01 Place the cucumber and mint in a medium mixing bowl.

02 Add the yogurt, lemon juice, salt, and pepper and stir to combine.

 Note: If using a variety of cucumber that has seeds or tough skin, seed and peel before grating. Persian, Armenian, and English cucumbers can be grated as-is.

cashew cream cheese

prep time: **5 minutes, plus 8 hours to soak the cashews and 12 to 18 hours to culture**
| makes: **about 1¼ cups**

While there may not be a substitute for real cream cheese, this comes pretty close. Culturing the puree gives it the cheesy tang that we all know and love. A good smear on some of my Seeded Crackers (page 251) with lox and chives has all the flavors of the bagel shop favorite, with added crunch.

2 cups raw cashews, soaked in 4 cups cold water for 8 to 12 hours

20 billion organisms probiotics (see Note)

1 tablespoon warm water

1 tablespoon lemon juice

½ teaspoon finely ground sea salt

¼ teaspoon cream of tartar

 Note: Probiotics can be purchased at your local health food or vitamin store. Be sure to purchase a brand that is in the refrigerated section.

01 After the cashews have soaked for at least 8 hours, drain them and place in a food processor or, better yet, a high-speed blender with a twister jar. (A high-speed blender will help you achieve the smooth texture you want more quickly than a food processor.)

02 Blend until smooth, scraping down the sides a few times. If you need to add a small amount of water to get it smooth, do so, but try to add as little water as possible while getting it as smooth as you possibly can.

03 Dissolve the probiotics in the tablespoon of warm (not hot) water and mix into the cashew mixture.

04 Line a fine-mesh strainer with cheesecloth and set over a bowl. Scrape the cashew mixture into it, then wrap the cheesecloth around and cover with a kitchen towel.

05 Allow to culture at room temperature for at least 12 hours. It will get more tart the longer you leave it. I tend to leave it for about 16 to 18 hours. You can taste it throughout the process and call it done when you like the taste.

06 After it is cultured to your liking, transfer the cheese to a bowl and stir in the lemon juice, salt, and cream of tartar.

07 Store in a glass jar in the refrigerator for up to 1 week.

balsamic redux

cook time: **10 to 15 minutes** | makes: **about ⅓ cup**

Having a jar of reduced balsamic vinegar on hand means you'll be ready to elevate just about any dish in a snap. Drizzle it on bitter greens such as arugula or radicchio for a dramatic salad, on grilled peaches for a simple and elegant dessert, or on roast chicken to give it a whole new flavor. It just happens to be good on ice cream, too.

1 cup balsamic vinegar

01 Bring the balsamic vinegar to a boil in a saucepan over medium-high heat.

02 Reduce the heat to low and simmer until the vinegar reduces to about ⅓ cup, 10 to 15 minutes. Make sure it doesn't burn. If it reduces too much, simply add a bit more vinegar or water to thin it out.

03 Allow to cool before transferring to a jar or bottle for storing. Reduced balsamic vinegar should keep indefinitely.

EGGS AND BREAKFAST

spinach, mushroom, and scallion frittata

prep time: **10 minutes** | cook time: **25 to 30 minutes** | serves: **4**

Frittatas are typically started on the stove and finished under the broiler, making them a quick and satisfying meal. Although still quick, my variation is a bit different: I cook the eggs at a lower temperature to ensure that they cook evenly all the way through without browning. This technique is especially helpful when cooking a large batch for a party, when they'll be cut it into bite-sized hors d'oeuvres.

9 large eggs

¾ teaspoon finely ground sea salt, divided

¼ teaspoon ground black pepper

1 tablespoon unsalted butter or ghee

½ pound cremini mushrooms, sliced ¼ inch thick

1 bunch spinach (about 10 ounces), stemmed and roughly chopped

1 bunch scallions, sliced

01 Preheat the oven to 300°F.

02 In a large bowl, beat the eggs with ½ teaspoon of the salt and the pepper.

03 Place a large cast iron skillet over medium-high heat and melt the butter.

04 Saute the mushrooms for 3 to 4 minutes, until golden brown and soft.

05 Add the remaining ¼ teaspoon of salt, the spinach, and the scallions. Stir until the spinach is wilted, about 1 minute.

06 Reduce the heat to medium, add the eggs, and allow to cook on the stove for 1 minute.

07 Place the skillet in the oven and cook for 20 to 25 minutes, or until the eggs are set.

08 Serve hot or at room temperature.

onion eggs

prep time: **5 minutes** | cook time: **15 minutes** | serves: **4**

Onion eggs are among the first foods that I remember from my childhood. They're almost too simple for a recipe, but they're far too delicious to be left out.

1 tablespoon unsalted butter, ghee, or preferred fat

1 small onion, cut into medium dice

8 large eggs

2 tablespoons heavy cream (see Note)

½ teaspoon finely ground sea salt

1 small bunch fresh chives, snipped into ¼-inch pieces

01 In a large skillet, melt the butter over medium-high heat.

02 Add the diced onion and saute for 2 minutes, or until golden brown and fragrant.

03 Turn the heat down to medium and continue cooking, stirring often, until the onions are soft and on their way to being caramelized, about 10 minutes.

04 Meanwhile, beat the eggs with the cream and salt.

05 Turn the heat up to medium-high and add the eggs to the pan.

06 Scramble the eggs to your liking, hard or soft or somewhere in between. (I grew up eating scrambled eggs on the well-done side and still love them that way, but a classically trained French chef would tell you to remove them from the heat before they're fully cooked to yield eggs that are soft and creamy.)

07 Remove from the heat and sprinkle with the chives.

 Note: Heavy cream adds a nice richness to the eggs, but if you avoid dairy, feel free to simply omit it.

silver dollar pancakes with blueberry compote

prep time: **10 minutes** | cook time: **25 to 30 minutes** | makes: **about 24 (3-inch) pancakes**

It's no secret that the average Paleo pancake could be used a weapon. Thanks to the many years I spent being a lazy jerk and watching my mom cook, I learned a valuable pancake lesson: beat the egg whites. (And based on that lesson, I'm pretty sure I also learned that being lazy pays.) When fluffy egg whites are folded into the batter, it aerates the pancakes and gives them some lift. The result? Fluffy pancakes!

For the compote

2½ cups frozen blueberries

½ cup orange juice

2 tablespoons honey

1 teaspoon unflavored gelatin

For the pancakes

8 large eggs, separated

2½ cups almond flour

½ cup arrowroot powder

1 teaspoon baking soda

½ teaspoon finely ground sea salt

⅓ cup heavy cream or full-fat coconut milk

6 tablespoons melted unsalted butter, ghee, or coconut oil

¼ cup honey or maple syrup

1 tablespoon vanilla extract

butter, ghee, or coconut oil, for the pan

01 Make the compote: In a small saucepan over medium heat, bring the blueberries and orange juice to a boil.

02 Stir in the honey and boil for 5 minutes, or until slightly thickened.

03 Remove the pan from the heat and allow to cool until it stops steaming.

04 Whisk in the gelatin. Allow to cool slightly before serving.

05 Make the pancakes: Beat the egg whites until stiff and set aside.

06 In a large mixing bowl, whisk together the almond flour, arrowroot, baking soda, and salt.

07 In a medium mixing bowl, beat the egg yolks, cream, melted butter, honey, and vanilla.

08 Pour the wet ingredients into the dry and stir until just combined.

09 Gently fold in the egg whites by using a large rubber spatula to bring the egg whites up and over the rest of the batter, while rotating the bowl, until combined. They will collapse a little, but by being gentle and using the folding method, you will keep them as whipped as possible.

10 Heat a large skillet over medium heat and melt a small amount of butter in it.

11 Pour the batter into the skillet in small amounts, about 2 tablespoons apiece. Cook for about 3 to 4 minutes and then flip. Adjust the heat as necessary; these take a bit longer to cook through than traditional pancakes, so you may need to lower the heat so they don't overcook on the bottom.

12 Flip and cook for another 2 to 3 minutes on the other side.

13 Keep warm in the oven while you cook the remaining batter.

eggs benedict

prep time: **10 minutes** | cook time: **15 minutes** | serves: **4**

Poached eggs have always been something that I love to eat but hate to make. I've tried every method and have never loved the results—until I tried the method that Michelle Tam features in her book *Food for Humans*. It turns out, all you need is a large slotted spoon and the freshest eggs you can find. No vinegar, no whirlpool, no special poaching equipment required.

1½ cups Lemony Hollandaise Sauce (page 62)

8 large eggs

4 Biscuits (page 240), warmed

8 thick slices Canadian bacon or ham

coarse sea salt

01 Bring a medium saucepan of water to a simmer. Adjust the heat so it's just producing tiny bubbles.

02 Crack open the eggs, one at a time, and drop each onto a large slotted spoon or fine-mesh strainer. Allow the loose strands of the whites to fall through; what remains on the spoon will be the yolk and the firm portion of the whites. You can drop the egg straight into the water at this point, or collect them in small bowls so they're all ready at once.

03 Drop the eggs into the water two at a time. Allow to poach until the whites are opaque, about 3 minutes. Remove with a slotted spoon. You can keep them warm in warm water as you make the rest.

04 Heat the Canadian bacon in a large skillet and keep warm.

05 To reheat the hollandaise: Place in a small pan over low heat and stir constantly. Add a tablespoon or two of hot water if it's too thick.

06 Slice open the biscuits and place a piece of Canadian bacon on each. Top with an egg and a spoonful of hollandaise. Sprinkle with coarse sea salt. Serve hot.

loaded banana bread

prep time: **10 minutes** | cook time: **50 to 55 minutes** | makes: **1 loaf**

I'm always on the hunt for the perfect portable breakfast bite. I know that sticking with whole foods such as meat and veggies is a better nutritional choice, but once in a while, it is both convenient and necessary to have a filling, nutrient-dense, and satisfying breakfast in the form of a slice of bread. This is exactly that. The bananas are sweet enough that no additional sweetener is required, and there's plenty of texture and contrast of flavors from the nuts, coconut, cacao nibs, and dried fruit.

1½ cups mashed very ripe bananas (about 3 bananas)

3 large eggs

¼ cup palm shortening or softened unsalted butter, plus more to grease the pan

1 tablespoon vanilla extract

1¼ cups almond flour

½ cup arrowroot powder

2 tablespoons coconut flour

1 teaspoon baking soda

¼ teaspoon finely ground sea salt

½ cup finely shredded unsweetened coconut

½ cup chopped raw pecans

¼ cup cacao nibs or mini dark chocolate chips

½ cup dried cherries or cranberries

01 Preheat the oven to 350°F. Grease a 7-inch loaf pan.

02 Combine the bananas, eggs, shortening, and vanilla in the bowl of a food processor or high-speed blender. Blend until well combined, about 20 seconds.

03 In a large bowl, combine the almond flour, arrowroot, coconut flour, baking soda, and salt.

04 Pour in the wet ingredients and stir to combine.

05 Stir in the coconut, pecans, cacao nibs, and cherries.

06 Pour into the prepared pan and bake for 50 to 55 minutes, or until a toothpick inserted into the middle comes out clean.

07 Allow to cool before removing from the pan.

blueberry muffins

prep time: **10 minutes** | cook time: **20 minutes** | makes: **12 muffins**

The classic all-American muffin, Paleo-ized. Of course blueberry season is an excellent time to make these, but frozen blueberries will work, too.

▶ **Make sure you have:** parchment muffin liners

¼ cup palm shortening or softened unsalted butter

4 large eggs

¼ cup honey

1 tablespoon vanilla extract

1¼ cups almond flour

½ cup arrowroot powder

2 tablespoons coconut flour

1 teaspoon baking soda

1¼ cups blueberries

01 Preheat the oven to 350°F and line a 12-cup muffin tin with parchment liners.

02 Add the shortening, eggs, honey, and vanilla to the bowl of a food processor and blend.

03 In a large bowl, whisk together the almond flour, arrowroot, coconut flour, and baking soda.

04 Pour the wet ingredients into the dry and stir to thoroughly combine.

05 Fold in the blueberries.

06 Divide the batter among the prepared muffin cups, filling them two-thirds full, and bake for 18 to 20 minutes, or until a toothpick inserted into the middle of a muffin comes out clean.

07 Cool in the muffin tin on a wire rack before removing from the pan.

apple spice muffins

prep time: **10 minutes** | cook time: **25 minutes** | makes: **12 muffins**

My first cooking job was an early-morning one: I was in charge of opening the restaurant. Before I was completely awake, I'd be making muffins, which included choosing the flavor of the day. I went with apple spice way too often, according to my bosses. It's still a favorite, especially in the fall, when apples are fresh off the trees and the smell of cinnamon and spice is just the thing you want filling your home.

▶ Make sure you have: parchment muffin liners

1 cup almond flour

½ cup arrowroot powder

2 tablespoons coconut flour

¼ cup plus 1 tablespoon coconut sugar, divided

2 teaspoons ground cinnamon, divided

¼ teaspoon ground nutmeg

⅛ teaspoon ground cloves

⅛ teaspoon ground cardamom

1 teaspoon baking soda

¼ teaspoon finely ground sea salt

3 eggs

¼ cup shortening or softened unsalted butter

1 teaspoon vanilla extract

2 medium Granny Smith apples

01 Preheat the oven to 350°F and line a 12-cup muffin tin with parchment liners.

02 In a large bowl, whisk together the almond flour, arrowroot, coconut flour, ¼ cup of the coconut sugar, 1 teaspoon of the cinnamon, the nutmeg, cloves, cardamom, baking soda, and salt.

03 In a medium bowl, beat together the eggs, shortening, and vanilla.

04 Peel and core the apples. Cut one into small dice, and grate the other.

05 Pour the wet ingredients into the dry and stir to combine. Mix in the grated and the diced apples.

06 In a small bowl, combine the remaining tablespoon of coconut sugar and the remaining teaspoon of cinnamon.

07 Divide the batter among the muffin cups, filling them two-thirds full, and sprinkle with the cinnamon sugar mixture.

08 Bake for 25 minutes, or until a toothpick inserted in the middle comes out clean. Allow to cool on a wire rack before removing from the pan.

chocolate hazelnut waffles

prep time: **10 minutes** | cook time: **5 to 10 minutes** | makes: **4 (8-inch) waffles**

What could be more indulgent than waffles on a Sunday morning? Well, chocolate hazelnut waffles, of course. Top them with strawberries and whipped cream or bananas sautéed in butter, or just eat them straight out of the waffle iron. (Maybe put them on a plate so you don't burn your fingers.)

1 cup raw hazelnuts

½ cup arrowroot powder

2 tablespoons cocoa powder

½ teaspoon baking soda

¼ teaspoon finely ground sea salt

4 large eggs

¼ cup heavy cream or full-fat coconut milk

3 tablespoons unsalted butter or coconut oil, melted

¼ cup honey

2 teaspoons vanilla extract

butter or coconut oil, for greasing the waffle iron

01 Preheat and grease the waffle iron.

02 In a food processor or high-speed blender, pulse the hazelnuts and arrowroot 7 to 8 times, or until it is a fine meal.

03 Add the cocoa powder, baking soda, and salt and pulse 2 to 3 times to incorporate.

04 In a large mixing bowl, beat the eggs with the cream, melted butter, honey, and vanilla.

05 Add the dry ingredients to the wet and stir to combine.

06 Pour a quarter of the batter into the heated waffle iron and cook for about 1 minute, depending on the efficiency of your waffle iron. The waffle should release easily when cooked through.

07 Repeat with the remaining batter three times, keeping the finished waffles in a warm oven.

sweet cinnamon cereal

prep time: **15 minutes** | cook time: **25 to 30 minutes** | makes: **about 3 cups**

I used to be a cereal-aholic. I wouldn't eat it for breakfast all that often, but I loved it as a late-night or mid-afternoon snack. While it's rare that I miss it these days, it's a nice treat once in a while.

1 egg

2 tablespoons honey

1 tablespoon melted coconut oil

1½ cups almond flour

½ cup tapioca starch

1 teaspoon coconut sugar

1 teaspoon ground cinnamon

Variation: This recipe can easily be made into graham crackers, too. Simply cut the dough into larger rectangles or into shapes with cookie cutters.

01 Preheat the oven to 350°F.

02 In a large bowl, whisk together the egg, honey, and melted coconut oil.

03 Add the almond flour and tapioca starch and knead to combine.

04 Turn the dough onto a sheet of parchment paper, flatten it a bit with your hands, and place another piece of parchment paper on top.

05 Roll out the dough to less than ⅛-inch thick, trying to get it as even as possible.

06 Score the dough into ½-inch squares, cutting all the way through (do not move the squares; you will break them apart later, after they are baked). Slide the dough and parchment paper onto a baking sheet and bake for 15 minutes.

07 Combine the coconut sugar and cinnamon in a small bowl and sprinkle over the dough, covering it as evenly as possible.

08 Turn the heat down to 325°F and bake for another 10 to 15 minutes, or until the cereal is crisp.

09 Allow to cool before breaking apart at the score marks.

STARTERS, SMALL BITES, AND PARTY FARE

chicken liver pâté

prep time: **10 minutes** | cook time: **20 minutes, plus time to chill** | makes: **2 cups**

This is the pâté that I serve to people who are somewhat liver-phobic. Chicken livers happen to be incredibly mild. When they're whipped into submission with sweet sherry, sautéed shallots, and thyme, they're tough not to love.

8 tablespoons unsalted butter, divided

1 cup sliced shallots (about 3 large)

1 pound organic chicken livers, tough membranes removed and patted dry

½ teaspoon finely ground sea salt

¼ teaspoon pepper

3 sprigs fresh thyme

½ cup dry sherry

01 Heat a large skillet over medium heat. Melt 2 tablespoons of the butter and add the shallots.

02 Saute the shallots for 5 minutes, or until golden brown and softened, stirring often.

03 Move the shallots to the perimeter of the pan and add the livers to the center. Cook 3 minutes per side, and sprinkle with the salt and pepper.

04 Add the sherry and thyme, turn the heat to medium-high, and bring to a simmer.

05 Cook until the liquid is almost gone, about 5 minutes.

06 Remove the thyme sprigs and transfer the liver mixture to a food processor. Turn it on and add the remaining butter 1 tablespoon at a time. Process until very smooth. Chill before serving.

 Serving suggestions

on Rosemary Crackers (page 249) with a slice of red grape

with Basic Crackers (page 248) and quince jam (available in the cheese sections of finer markets) or a slice of fresh ripe pear

with Bread Sticks (page 244) and cornichons

oysters rockefeller

prep time: **10 minutes** | cook time: **15 minutes** | serves: **4 to 6**

Oysters tend to be a "love 'em or hate 'em" type of food. I am certainly an oyster lover, but I understand the aversion some have to them. For people who are on the fence, allow me to present to you the gateway oyster. With crispy, salty bacon, flavorful herbs, and a quick blast in the oven, even oyster haters are likely to give these a try.

2 strips thick-cut bacon, cut into lardons (¼-inch strips)

1 tablespoon unsalted butter or bacon fat

1 teaspoon fennel seeds

3 scallions, thinly sliced, white and light green parts only

2 cloves garlic, minced

1 cup packed watercress leaves (about 1 bunch), chopped

¼ cup packed fresh parsley leaves, minced

3 sprigs fresh lemon thyme, or regular thyme plus ½ teaspoon finely grated lemon zest

2 cups kosher salt

12 to 20 fresh oysters on the half shell, depending on size, shucked (see Note)

lemon wedges, for serving

hot sauce, for serving

01 Preheat the oven to 425°F.

02 Cook the bacon in a small skillet over medium heat until crispy, about 5 minutes. Remove the bacon from the pan and drain on paper towels.

03 Melt the butter in the pan over medium heat. Add the fennel seeds, scallions, and garlic. Saute for 20 to 30 seconds, until fragrant. Remove from heat and add the watercress, parsley, and thyme.

04 Pour the salt into a large baking dish and place the oysters on top. Spoon 1 to 2 teaspoons of the herb mix onto each one. Top with the bacon and bake for 8 to 10 minutes, until hot.

05 Serve with lemon wedges and hot sauce.

 Note: Ask your fishmonger to shuck the oysters for you if you don't have a shucking knife and protective gloves.

spiced pepitas

prep time: **5 minutes** | cook time: **5 to 7 minutes** | makes: **about 1½ cups**

It's on the table at almost every party—the bowl of spiced nuts. I'm finding that more and more people around me are allergic to nuts, so I wanted to create a tasty snack alternative for them. These spiced pepitas also are phenomenal sprinkled on salads, add a nice crunch to tacos, and are great on soup.

1½ cups raw pumpkin seeds

1 tablespoon lemon, orange, or lime juice

¾ teaspoon finely ground sea salt

⅛ teaspoon ground cinnamon

⅛ teaspoon chipotle powder

½ teaspoon ground cumin

½ teaspoon ground coriander

¼ teaspoon smoked paprika

1 teaspoon coconut sugar (see Note)

01 Preheat the oven to 375°F and line a baking sheet with parchment paper.

02 In a medium bowl, mix together the pumpkin seeds, lemon juice, salt, cinnamon, chipotle powder, cumin, coriander, smoked paprika, and coconut sugar.

03 Spread on the prepared baking sheet and bake for 5 to 7 minutes, or until crisp and puffed. Allow to cool before storing in an airtight container. They'll keep for weeks, but if they lose some of their crunch, you can reheat them in a 350°F oven for 2 to 3 minutes.

 Note: If you'e doing a sugar detox, just omit the sugar.

plantain shoestring fries

prep time: **15 minutes** | cook time: **20 minutes** | serves: **4**

Crispy, salty, fun to eat . . . These might be what you need to rid yourself of those potato chip cravings forever. While they're a wonderful snack on their own, they're also great as a crunchy topper for Mango-Chile Ceviche (page 102) and add the perfect crunch to Tortilla Soup (page 138).

▶ **Make sure you have:** a julienne peeler (it works better than a spiral slicer for this recipe)

1 cup coconut oil

2 green plantains

finely ground sea salt

01 Heat the oil to 350°F to 365°F in a medium heavy-bottomed saucepan. (You want plenty of space above the oil, so err on the side of a larger pan.)

02 Cut off the tops and bottoms of the plantains and score the peel lengthwise 3 or 4 times. Remove the peel.

03 Julienne the plantains with a julienne peeler. Slice the plantains in half first if you don't want the fries to be super long.

04 Working in several batches, drop a handful of julienned plantain into the hot oil. Fry for 3 to 4 minutes, or until crispy. Use tongs to carefully move them around a bit as they cook.

05 Remove to several layers of paper towels and shower with salt immediately.

mango-chile ceviche

prep time: **15 minutes** | cook time: **2 to 3 hours to marinate** | serves: **4 to 8**

Ceviche might just be the perfect dish to prepare on a hot summer day. You don't need to turn on the stove, even for a second, and the end result is a clean and brightly flavored satisfying dish. Make sure to use the freshest fish you can find, and make the ceviche on the same day you buy the fish. My favorite way to serve this is topped with Avocado Mousse (page 50) and Plantain Shoestring Fries (page 100).

1 large mango, cut into small dice (about ¾ cup)

½ cup diced cucumber (about 1 small)

¼ cup finely diced sweet onion

1 to 2 tablespoons minced jalapeño pepper or red chile

¼ cup fresh cilantro leaves, roughly chopped

1 pound wild tai snapper, rockfish, or other mild, firm-flesh fish fillets, skin removed (see Note)

½ cup lemon juice

½ cup lime juice

1 teaspoon finely ground sea salt

dash of hot sauce, or more to taste (or serve it on the side, if preferred)

Avocado Mousse (page 50), for serving

Plantain Shoestring Fries (page 100), for serving

01 Place the mango, cucumber, onion, jalapeño, and cilantro in a large glass or ceramic bowl.

02 Cut the fish into medium dice and place it in the bowl with the other ingredients.

03 Pour in the lemon and lime juice and the salt. Stir to combine.

04 Allow to sit for 2 to 3 hours, covered and refrigerated.

05 Serve with hot sauce, Avocado Mousse, and Plantain Shoestring Fries.

 Note: If you are not comfortable removing the skin of the fish yourself, ask your fishmonger to do it for you.

steak tartare

prep time: **45 minutes** | serves: **4 to 8**

It's no surprise that tartare fell out of fashion for quite some time. A quick Google search will bring up hundreds of pictures of what looks to be a hamburger that someone forgot to cook. The key to good tartare is simple: Use the best beef and eggs you can find, keep the rest of the ingredients simple and restrained, and hand-mince the meat.

1 pound Châteaubriand or filet mignon (see Note)

2 egg yolks, beaten

1 tablespoon Dijon mustard

1 tablespoon capers, rinsed and drained

1 tablespoon extra virgin olive oil

2 tablespoons minced shallots

2 teaspoons Worcestershire sauce

1 teaspoon minced anchovies, or anchovy paste

½ teaspoon white wine vinegar

¼ teaspoon finely ground sea salt

⅛ teaspoon cayenne pepper

⅛ teaspoon ground black pepper

2 tablespoons minced fresh parsley

endive leaves and cornichons, for serving

01 Place the steak in the freezer for 30 minutes to get it very cold.

02 Meanwhile, prep the remainder of the ingredients and mix them together in a large bowl.

03 Mince the meat into ⅛- to ¼-inch pieces with a very sharp knife. A carving knife is best, but a chef's knife will work, too.

04 Mix the beef with the other ingredients.

05 To serve, press into a ring mold, if you have one, or simply place it on a somewhat even shape on a cold plate. Serve with endive leaves and cornichons.

 Note: Châteaubriand is a cut of beef from the center of the tenderloin. It is just as tender as filet mignon, and is often even more flavorful, too. The best part? It's considerably less expensive than filet mignon.

coconut shrimp with clementine-chili dipping sauce

prep time: **15 minutes** | cook time: **15 minutes** | serves: **4 to 6**

For the love of coconut. And succulent shrimp. And the perfect crispy texture.

For the dipping sauce

2 clementines, peeled

2 tablespoons coconut aminos

¼ cup honey

2 tablespoons Sriracha sauce (see Note)

For the shrimp

2 cups coconut oil, for frying

1 cup tapioca starch

½ teaspoon finely ground sea salt

¼ teaspoon cayenne pepper

¼ teaspoon ground white pepper

2 egg whites

1 cup finely shredded unsweetened coconut

1 pound large shrimp (with tails on), peeled and deveined

 Note: Look for the Organicville brand of Sriracha sauce, which has cleaner ingredients, or make your own if you're feeling adventurous. You'll find a fantastic recipe in *Food for Humans* by Michelle Tam and Henry Fong.

01 Make the dipping sauce: Place the ingredients for the sauce in a blender and blend until smooth. Transfer to a small saucepan and cook over medium heat for 4 to 5 minutes, or until thickened. Remove to a small serving bowl.

02 Preheat the frying oil: Heat a large, heavy pot over medium heat and melt the coconut oil. Heat the oil to 350°F. (If you don't have a thermometer, you can test the temperature of the oil by dropping a few shreds of coconut in it; if they sizzle immediately, the oil is ready.)

03 Prepare the shrimp: Set out three shallow bowls. In the first one, mix together the tapioca starch, salt, cayenne pepper, and white pepper.

04 In the second bowl, whisk the egg whites until they're frothy.

05 In the third bowl, pour in the shredded coconut.

06 Grabbing the shrimp by their tails, dredge them first in the tapioca mixture, then in the egg whites, then in the coconut.

07 Once they're all coated, drop them into the hot oil, about 6 to 8 at a time, making sure not to crowd them.

08 Fry for 2 to 3 minutes per side, until golden brown. Remove to a wire rack to drain. Keep warm in the oven while you fry the remaining batches. Serve hot with the dipping sauce.

maple-bourbon bacon jam

prep time: **10 minutes** | cook time: **2 to 2½ hours** | makes: **about 4 cups**

Does bacon jam really need an introduction? Not really. It's bacon jam. You can put it on Basic Crackers (page 248), with cherry tomatoes and arugula, top a burger with it, spread it on a Biscuit (page 240). And no judgments if you just eat it with a spoon.

1 pound bacon, roughly chopped

1 large onion, cut into large dice

¾ cup brewed coffee (decaf is fine)

⅓ cup maple syrup

¼ cup apple cider vinegar

3 tablespoons bourbon

01 Preheat the oven to 300°F.

02 In a Dutch oven, brown the bacon on medium-low heat until it is brown and has rendered a good amount of fat, about 20 minutes.

03 Remove the bacon from the pot with a slotted spoon and pour off the majority of the fat, leaving only about a tablespoon of fat in the pot.

04 Add the onion to the pot and sauté it over medium heat until it is golden brown and softened, about 10 minutes.

05 Add the coffee, maple syrup, apple cider vinegar, bourbon, and bacon to the pot and bring to a simmer.

06 Place the pot in the oven and cook, covered, for 1 hour.

07 Carefully remove the pot from the oven and give the contents a stir. Return it to the oven, checking every 30 minutes, until the liquid has thickened to a syrupy consistency. Keep in mind it will thicken more once it cools, so you want it to still be a little loose.

08 Allow to cool for 15 to 20 minutes.

09 Transfer to the bowl of a food processor and pulse 6 to 8 times, until it's an even consistency but not yet pureed.

10 Store in glass jars in the refrigerator for up to 2 weeks.

two-bite flatbreads

prep time: **10 minutes, plus 90 minutes to make the dough** | cook time: **10 minutes** | makes: **about 24 squares**

When you've got a vehicle for toppings, your hors d'oeuvre options are virtually endless! Here are some tried-and-true combos that are surefire crowd-pleasers.

1 batch Pizza Crust dough (page 242)

Topping ideas

fig jam, prosciutto, shaved Parmesan cheese

Maple-Bourbon Bacon Jam (page 108), arugula, cherry tomatoes

pesto, cooked crumbled sausage, sliced roasted bell pepper

diced tomato, sliced fresh mozzarella, chiffonaded fresh basil leaves

shredded Cocoa-Chili Pork Shoulder (page 190), sliced jalapeño peppers, finely diced pineapple

01 Preheat the oven to 500°F.

02 Form the dough into two, three, or four rectangles, depending on how many varieties of flatbread you plan to make.

03 Bake for 6 to 8 minutes, or until it just starts to brown on the edges.

04 Turn the oven down to 425°F.

05 Top with desired toppings, and bake another 2 to 3 minutes.

06 Allow to rest for 1 to 2 minutes before cutting into 1½-inch squares.

SOUPS AND SALADS

roasted beet and orange salad

prep time: **15 minutes** | cook time: **90 minutes** | serves: **4**

Seasonal produce can start to seem a bit sparse come the middle of winter, and this salad is just the thing to beat the winter blahs. Not only is it dramatically colorful, the balance of earthy, sweet, and bitter will snap your taste buds right into spring.

1 pound beets (about 5 medium)

2 tablespoons light olive oil

finely ground sea salt

1 cup shredded endive (about 1 head)

½ cup shaved fennel bulb (about 1 small bulb) plus 2 tablespoons of roughly chopped fennel frond tips, for garnish (optional)

1 medium orange, preferably cara cara or blood

Blood Orange Vinaigrette (page 52), for serving

01 Preheat the oven to 425°F.

02 Wrap each beet in its own aluminum foil purse, leaving the top open. Into each beet package, add about 1 teaspoon olive oil and a pinch of salt. Pinch the purses closed.

03 Place the beets in a small roasting pan and roast them for about 90 minutes, or until they give a bit when you squeeze them. Carefully open up the purses (watch out for escaping steam).

04 Once the beets are cool enough to handle, rub the peels off. Slice horizontally in rounds.

05 To assemble the salad: Arrange the endive and fennel on four plates and top with the beets and oranges. Drizzle with the vinaigrette and garnish with the fennel fronds, if desired.

persimmon salad with grapes, prosciutto, and almonds

prep time: **15 minutes** | serves: **4**

This is the perfect fall salad to serve as the first course at a dinner party. It's got sweetness from the fruit, saltiness from the prosciutto, and just a touch of bitter from the radicchio— just the thing to get your guests' appetites going. If serving family style, simply tear the prosciutto into pieces and toss the ingredients together, instead of following the plating instructions below.

8 slices prosciutto

1 small head radicchio (about 4 ounces)

4 ounces baby spinach

3 to 4 tablespoons Champagne Vinaigrette (page 53)

4 ounces grapes, halved

2 Fuyu persimmons, sliced thin

¼ cup sliced almonds

01 On each of four salad plates, place two slices of prosciutto.

02 Roughly chop the radicchio and place it in a large bowl, along with the baby spinach, and toss with the vinaigrette.

03 Divide the dressed greens among the plates.

04 Divide the halved grapes and sliced persimmons on top of the greens and sprinkle with the almonds.

 If you can't get persimmons in your neck of the woods, this salad is equally lovely with perfectly ripe pears.

kabocha squash and pomegranate salad

prep time: **10 minutes** | cook time: **20 minutes** | serves: **4 to 6**

Kabocha squash roasts up quickly when sliced thin, and the skin is tender enough to eat. This salad makes for a gorgeous celebration of fall, worthy of a place on your Thanksgiving table.

½ pound kabocha squash

1 tablespoon coconut oil, melted, or preferred fat

4 ounces arugula

½ cup pomegranate arils (seeds), from about 1 pomegranate

½ cup toasted walnuts

¼ cup Spiced Pepitas (page 98)

Champagne Vinaigrette (page 53), for serving

 To remove the arils from the pomegranate: Slice the the pomegranate in half lengthwise. Hold one half in your hand, cut side down, over a bowl of water. With a wooden spoon, firmly whack the outside of the pomegranate all over, allowing the arils and white pith to fall into the water. The pith will rise to the top, making it easy to remove and discard. The arils will sink to the bottom, so all you have to do is drain and use. There will likely be some juice splatter, so don't do this wearing your favorite white shirt!

01 Preheat the oven to 425°F.

02 Cut off the tops and bottoms of the squash with a sharp knife and then cut in half. Scoop out the seeds and place the squash halves flesh side down on a cutting board. Slice into ¼-inch half-moons.

03 In a large bowl, toss the squash with the melted coconut oil until it's well coated.

04 Transfer to a rimmed baking sheet and roast for 10 minutes.

05 Flip the squash and roast for 10 minutes more, or until tender and brown on the edges.

06 Allow to cool a bit before arranging the salad.

07 To plate the salad, arrange the arugula on a large serving platter and top with the roasted squash, pomegranate arils, toasted walnuts, and spiced pepitas.

08 Drizzle with the vinaigrette, or serve it on the side for guests to help themselves.

summer salad
with padron peppers

prep time: **10 minutes** | cook time: **20 minutes** | serves: **6 to 8**

This salad involves a bit more prep than simply chopping veggies, but it's worth it! The colors, textures, and bright flavors practically scream summertime. It is just the thing to bring to a potluck or to serve as a light lunch or dinner with some grilled chicken or fish.

10 to 12 pearl onions (see Notes)

3 tablespoons light olive oil or ghee, divided

1 cup padron peppers (see Notes)

coarse sea salt

1 pound heirloom tomatoes, cherry tomatoes, or a combination

½ pound cucumbers (Persian, Armenian, or any seedless variety)

2 small or 1 large bell pepper (red, orange, purple, or yellow)

1 cup olives, Kalamata or Castelvetrano

For the dressing

¼ cup extra virgin olive oil

2 tablespoons lemon juice, preferably Meyer

1 teaspoon Dijon mustard

2 tablespoons chopped fresh parsley

01 Set a small saucepan of water over medium heat and bring to a boil. Add the whole pearl onions and blanch for 2 minutes.

02 Strain and plunge into a bowl of cold water. Once they're cool enough to handle, remove the skins.

03 Place the onions along with 1 tablespoon of the olive oil in a small saucepan and cook on medium-low heat for 8 to 10 minutes, stirring often, until golden. Add a tablespoon of water and cover for 1 to 2 minutes. Remove from heat and set aside.

04 In a small skillet, heat the remaining 2 tablespoons of olive oil over medium-high heat and sauté the padron peppers (whole with stem on) until blistered and soft, about 5 minutes. Remove from pan and sprinkle with coarse sea salt.

05 Dice the tomatoes, cucumbers, and bell pepper into bite-sized pieces. Arrange on a serving platter.

06 Add the olives, padron peppers, and onions.

07 In a small bowl, whisk together the ingredients for dressing. Drizzle over the salad immediately before serving.

Notes: If the pearl onion process is more than you're up for, feel free to substitute a small red onion, thinly sliced, or thickly sliced and sautéed quickly over high heat to give it a bit of extra flavor.

Padron peppers are small, light green peppers that have just a little bit of a kick. They are commonly seen on tapas menus and are sautéed in olive oil and sprinkled with coarse sea salt. Look for them in the spring, when they make a brief appearance at farmers markets.

raw kale salad with currants and pine nuts

prep time: **15 minutes** | serves: **4**

Once in a while, my mom calls me and says "do this." To make up for all those teenage years when I did the opposite of whatever she told me to do, I listen. This recipe is the result of one of those phone calls. Back when kale was just becoming as popular as spinach, she told me about this recipe, in which the kale is massaged instead of cooked and is combined with a few complementary ingredients for outstanding flavor and texture.

¼ cup pine nuts (see Note)

¼ cup balsamic vinegar

¼ cup currants

2 bunches Lacinato kale (also called dinosaur kale; about 1¼ pounds)

¼ cup extra virgin olive oil

¼ teaspoon finely ground sea salt

2 tablespoons lemon juice

01 Heat a small skillet over medium-low heat and add the pine nuts. Toast for 2 to 3 minutes, stirring often. Make sure they don't burn. Once they are fragrant, remove from the pan and set aside.

02 To the same pan, add the balsamic vinegar and currants. Once steaming, turn off the heat. Allow to sit while you prepare the kale.

03 Pull the leaves off the stems of the kale, roll up the leaves lengthwise, and chiffonade as thinly as possible (see page 34).

04 In a large bowl, massage the kale with the olive oil for 3 to 5 minutes, or until it's reduced by one-third to one-half.

05 Stir in the salt, currants, balsamic vinegar, lemon juice, and pine nuts.

 Note: If not serving right away, keep the pine nuts separate so they don't lose their crunch.

jicama slaw

prep time: **15 minutes** | serves: **4**

It wasn't until I moved to California that I tried jicama, and I have no idea how I ever lived without it. The brown, papery exterior gives no indication of the incredible juicy crispness that awaits inside.

3 tablespoons lime juice

1 teaspoons apple cider vinegar

¼ cup extra virgin olive oil

1 teaspoon honey

½ teaspoon finely ground sea salt

1 softball-sized jicama, peeled and julienned

1 bell pepper (red, orange or yellow), cored and julienned

1 bunch scallions, thinly sliced

¼ cup minced fresh cilantro

01 In a medium bowl, mix together the lime juice, vinegar, olive oil, honey, and salt.

02 Add the jicama, bell pepper, scallions, and cilantro and stir to combine.

03 Serve cold.

creamy purple cabbage slaw

prep time: **15 minutes** | serves: **4**

Slaw isn't exactly a major culinary breakthrough, but like most things delicious, it's about the balance of flavors and textures. Crispy cabbage mixed with a dressing that is creamy, tangy, sweet, and a little bit tart, is something that is greater than the sum of its parts.

¾ cup Mayonnaise (page 54)

2 tablespoons white wine vinegar

1 tablespoon honey

½ teaspoon celery seed

¾ teaspoon finely ground sea salt

⅛ teaspoon ground black pepper

1 small red cabbage (about 1 pound), shredded

2 tablespoons grated red onion

3 carrots, peeled or scrubbed and grated

01   In a large bowl, mix together the mayonnaise, vinegar, honey, celery seed, salt, and pepper.

02   Add the cabbage, onion, and carrot and stir to combine. Serve cold.

rich chicken broth

prep time: **15 minutes** | cook time: **2 to 3 hours** (pressure cooker); **4 to 4½ hours** (stockpot) | makes: **3 to 4 quarts**

In a perfect world, I would always have at least a quart of this in the fridge or freezer. Aside from being one of the healthiest things you can sip out of a mug, it's the ideal base for countless soups and just the thing to add to braises.

5 to 6 pounds meaty chicken bones (preferably 4 pounds backs, 1 pound necks, and ½ to 1 pound feet)

1½ tablespoons apple cider vinegar

1 teaspoon finely ground sea salt

3 to 4 quarts cold, filtered water

2 pounds carrots, roughly chopped

1 pound parsnips, roughly chopped

1 large onion, roughly chopped

1 pound celery, roughly chopped

1 pound celery root, peeled and roughly chopped

6 to 8 cloves garlic

For added nutrient density (optional)

1 (12-inch) piece kombu, well rinsed, and/or eggshells (added with the bones)

1 bunch fresh parsley or other fresh herbs (added with the veggies)

 Variation: For beef or pork broth, the technique is the same; simply swap out the chicken bones for beef or pork knuckle bones. If using a stockpot instead of a pressure cooker, increase the initial cooking time to 4 to 5 hours.

01 Place the chicken bones, apple cider vinegar, and salt in your pressure cooker or large stockpot.

02 Add the water, cover, and bring up to pressure (or a boil if using a stockpot) over high heat.

03 Once the pressure valve pops, turn the burner down to the lowest possible heat to keep the valve popped. If using a stockpot, bring down to a simmer and cover.

04 If using a pressure cooker: Allow to cook for at least 1 hour, up to 1½ hours. If using a stockpot: Simmer for at least 3 hours for good flavor, and longer if you want to get more minerals out of the bones.

05 Uncover the pressure cooker or stockpot and add the vegetables and garlic. Bring to a boil and reduce, uncovered, for 1 to 1½ hours, until the vegetables are very soft.

06 Strain the broth, getting as much liquid out of the ingredients as possible. Pour into jars. Once the fat rises to the top, plunge a small ladle into the jar to remove and discard it, or save it for future use.

07 Store the broth for up to 1 week in the fridge or up to 6 weeks in the freezer.

hot and sour soup

prep time: **10 minutes** | cook time: **40 minutes** | serves: **4 to 6**

Even though I grew up in a Jewish family with chicken soup making an appearance at every holiday, this soup is the one I remember most from my childhood. My dad was a Chinese food enthusiast and made this soup often. He still brags about the fact that I ate super spicy hot and sour soup at eighteen months old. (I might have been an odd child.) Hot and sour soup is an ancient Chinese remedy, an immune-boosting powerhouse. With a base of chicken broth (aka Jewish penicillin), the astringency of vinegar, and the antiviral properties of black mushrooms and lily buds, it's the perfect thing to whip up when you're feeling a bit under the weather.

½ cup dried Chinese black mushrooms

24 dried lily buds, tough ends cut off and quartered lengthwise (see Note)

2 quarts Chicken or Pork Broth (page 128)

1 (4-by-6-inch) piece kombu, rinsed

1 (2-inch) piece ginger, peeled and grated

1 teaspoon ground white pepper

¼ cup coconut aminos

¼ cup coconut vinegar

2 tablespoons arrowroot powder

¼ cup cold water

2 large eggs, beaten

1 tablespoon toasted sesame oil

½ cup sliced scallions, for garnish

chili oil, for garnish (optional)

01 Place the dried mushrooms and lily buds in a large bowl and cover with boiling water. Set aside to reconstitute. Once the mushrooms are soft enough to cut, drain the liquid and slice them thinly.

02 Heat the broth in a large soup pot over medium heat and add the rinsed kombu and grated ginger. Simmer for 20 to 30 minutes. Remove the kombu and discard.

03 Add the rehydrated and sliced mushrooms, rehydrated lily buds, white pepper, coconut aminos, and coconut vinegar and simmer for 5 minutes.

04 In a small bowl, combine the arrowroot with the ¼ cup cold water and stir to make a slurry.

05 Pour the slurry into the soup and simmer an additional 5 minutes.

06 While stirring, slowly pour in the beaten eggs.

07 Add the toasted sesame oil and turn off the heat.

08 Serve garnished with sliced scallions and a drizzle of chili oil, if desired.

▶ Traditional hot and sour soup recipes include pork, but I prefer to go heavier on the mushrooms and lily buds instead. If you would like to add it, follow the instructions for marinating, cooking, and slicing the pork used in BBQ Pork Pho (page 132).

 Note: Lily buds are the dried, unopened flowers of day lilies. They have been used in China as both food and medicine for over 2,000 years and are said to settle a cough and help with insomnia. You'll find them in an Asian market or online. Make sure to purchase ones that are bendable and not too brittle.

bbq pork pho

prep time: **1 hour** | cook time: **1 hour** | serves: **4 to 6**

When I first moved to San Francisco, I wandered into a Vietnamese restaurant in my neighborhood to get some lunch before signing my lease. The menu was long and I was an East Coast transplant, not an expert on Vietnamese food by any means. I asked the owner what I should order, and he pointed to the BBQ pork pho and the fresh rolls. I kid you not, I have ordered the exact same thing every time I've been back.

For the marinade

2 tablespoons coconut aminos

2 tablespoons fish sauce

1 tablespoon honey (optional)

For the soup

1 pound boneless thin pork chops (about ½ inch thick)

1 large onion

1 (4-inch) piece ginger

2 quarts Beef or Pork Broth (page 128)

2 cinnamon sticks

5 whole cloves

5 star anise

8 zucchini (2½ to 3 pounds)

2 tablespoons coconut aminos

¼ cup fish sauce

For the garnishes

1 (6-inch) piece daikon radish

1 jalapeño pepper

1 small bunch fresh basil, Thai if available

1 small bunch fresh mint

1 lime, cut into wedges

01 In a small bowl, mix together the marinade ingredients. Pour the marinade into a resealable bag or glass container and add the pork. Set the pork aside to marinate at room temperature for up to an hour. Refrigerate if you plan on marinating it longer.

02 Preheat the broiler to high. Move a rack to the upper position.

03 Peel the onion and slice into 6 wedges. Cut the ginger into 1-inch pieces.

04 Broil the onion and ginger for 15 minutes, turning frequently, until charred.

05 Heat the broth in a large pot over medium heat.

06 Add the charred onions and ginger to the broth. For easy removal, wrap the cinnamon, cloves, and star anise in a piece of cheesecloth, secure with butcher's twine, and add to the broth. Simmer for 45 minutes, then remove the onion, ginger, and spices. Discard.

07 While the soup simmers, prepare the rest of the ingredients: Preheat the grill to medium-high or a grill pan over medium-high heat. Remove the pork from the marinade and pat dry. If your grill or grill pan isn't well seasoned, lightly grease it.

08 Grill the pork for 2 to 3 minutes per side, or until cooked through. Remove and slice into thin strips.

09 Using a spiral slicer or julienne peeler, make long noodles out of the zucchini and daikon. Set the daikon on a serving platter; set the zucchini aside.

10 Slice the jalapeño into thin rounds and place it on the platter with the daikon. Add the basil, mint, and lime wedges to the platter.

11 After the soup has simmered for a total of 45 minutes, add the 2 tablespoons of coconut aminos and ¼ cup of fish sauce. Simmer a few minutes more.

12 Into each bowl, place a quarter of the zucchini noodles and pork. Ladle the broth on top.

13 Serve the bowls of soup with the garnishes for people to assemble themselves.

chicken soup

prep time: **10 minutes** | cook time: **10 minutes** | serves: **6 to 8**

Every holiday with my family started with chicken soup. It was always mostly broth, so the person making the soup was under a lot of pressure to get it perfect. This version is heartier than the first-course bowls I grew up with, but it still depends on a richly flavored broth. While store-bought stocks can sometimes work in a pinch for certain recipes, they just won't cut it for this one. Make sure to adjust your prep time accordingly if you don't have a roast chicken and homemade broth on hand.

3 quarts Chicken Broth (page 128)

4 to 5 carrots (¾ pound), peeled or scrubbed and cut into small dice

3 to 4 parsnips (¾ pound), peeled and cut into small dice

1 small bunch fresh parsley

1 small bunch fresh dill

1 whole Perfect Roast Chicken (page 158)

01 Heat the chicken broth in a large pot over medium heat. Add the vegetables and herbs and simmer for 5 minutes, or until tender.

02 Meanwhile, shred the chicken, using your hands if it's cool enough to handle, two forks if not. Discard the skin.

03 Once the vegetables are soft, remove the herbs and add the chicken. Simmer another minute, or until heated through.

 This version of chicken soup represents my perfect bowl. Feel free to add your own favorites! Celery, peas, root veggies, and sweet potatoes are all good additions. You can also add your preferred herbs.

roasted cauliflower soup with lime and pine nuts

prep time: **15 minutes** | cook time: **40 to 50 minutes** | serves: **4 to 6**

Anytime I write a menu for a catering job, I have *The Flavor Bible* by my side. It is my most prized cooking resource, an actual dictionary of flavor combinations for just about every ingredient you can imagine. This soup is a result of that book. Never would I have thought of pairing lime and cauliflower, but ever since I have, this soup been a client favorite and has made an appearance on many menus.

1 head cauliflower (about 2 pounds), cut into thick slices (no need to core it)

1 large onion, peeled and cut into thick slices

2 tablespoons unsalted butter, duck fat, or preferred cooking fat, melted

3 tablespoons pine nuts

1 quart Chicken Broth (page 128), plus more if needed

1 teaspoon finely ground sea salt

¼ teaspoon ground black pepper

2 tablespoons lime juice

grated zest of 1 lime

01 Preheat the oven to 450°F.

02 Toss the cauliflower and onion with the melted butter on a rimmed baking sheet and roast for 30 to 35 minutes, turning the vegetables halfway through.

03 Toast the pine nuts in a small, dry pan on medium-low heat for 3 to 5 minutes, flipping them often. They will start releasing their oils and then start to brown. Once they start browning, remove them from the pan and set aside.

04 Transfer the roasted vegetables to a stockpot and pour in just enough broth to cover the vegetables. Pour a small amount of broth onto the roasting pan and scrape with a spatula to release any stuck-on bits. Add that liquid to the stockpot as well. Bring to a simmer and cook for 10 to 15 minutes, until the cauliflower is very soft.

05 Transfer the soup to a blender and puree until smooth, adding more broth as needed to obtain the desired texture.

06 Add the salt and pepper, then taste for seasoning and add more salt if needed, ¼ teaspoon at a time.

07 Before serving, squeeze in the lime juice and garnish with the lime zest and pine nuts.

tortilla soup

prep time: **20 minutes** | cook time: **40 minutes** | serves: **4**

I've been the soup lady at just about every restaurant I've worked at, and this soup has always been in the rotation. The balance of flavors is sublime: smoky, spicy, and complex. The soup can very well stand alone without any additions, but the garnishes make it fun and festive. Plantain Shoestring Fries (page 100) are the perfect replacement for the corn tortilla chips that are typically found in tortilla soup.

2 bell peppers, roasted (red, orange, or yellow, or a combination; see Note, page 58)

1 tablespoon lard, coconut oil, or duck fat

1 medium onion, cut into medium dice

4 cloves garlic, sliced

1 teaspoon finely ground sea salt

1 teaspoon ground cumin

1 teaspoon ground coriander

2 teaspoons smoked paprika

½ teaspoon ground chipotle powder

1 (14-ounce) jar diced tomatoes or 2 cups fresh

1 quart Chicken Broth (page 128)

2 cups shredded cooked chicken

For serving

2 avocados, diced

1 lime, quartered

1 small handful fresh cilantro leaves

Plantain Shoestring Fries (page 100)

01 Core and seed the roasted bell peppers and cut them into small dice. Set aside.

02 Heat a large soup pot over medium-high heat and add the lard.

03 Sauté the onion for 12 to 15 minutes, stirring occasionally, until softened and browned. Add the garlic and cook for 1 more minute.

04 Add the salt, cumin, coriander, smoked paprika, and chipotle powder and cook for another 30 seconds, stirring constantly.

05 Add the tomatoes, broth, and roasted peppers and bring to a boil. Turn the heat down to medium-low and simmer, uncovered, for 25 to 30 minutes.

06 Add the shredded chicken and cook another minute, or until heated though.

07 To serve, garnish each bowl with one-quarter of the diced avocado, a lime wedge, cilantro leaves, and a small handful of plantain fries.

Having a party? Make a big batch of this and offer additional garnishes for guests to top their bowls with. Grilled shrimp, queso fresco, grilled tomatillos, and sliced jalapeños are just a few ideas.

FISH AND SEAFOOD

grilled sardines

prep time: **20 minutes, plus 30 minutes to marinate** | cook time: **10 minutes** | serves: **4**

It's too bad that so many people dislike sardines, as they are some of the healthiest, and least expensive, fish there are. If you've only had the canned variety, I urge you to give these a try. I think you might be pleasantly surprised by how well the smokiness of the grill and tartness of the lemon complements them.

1½ pounds whole sardines (about 4 large), gutted (see Note)

1 teaspoon coarse sea salt

For the marinade and dressing

1 tablespoon extra virgin olive oil

2 tablespoons minced fresh parsley

grated zest of 1 lemon

¼ cup fresh lemon juice (1 to 2 lemons)

½ teaspoon finely ground sea salt

1 clove garlic, minced

01 Rinse the gutted sardines well under cold water and pat dry.

02 In a small bowl, combine the olive oil, parsley, lemon zest, lemon juice, and the finely ground salt.

03 Pour half of the lemon mixture into a baking dish that will fit the sardines in a single layer. (Set the other half of the mixture aside; you will use it to dress the grilled sardines.) Add the garlic to the baking dish and stir to mix into the marinade. Add the sardines and coat with the marinade, making sure to get some inside the fish as well. Cover and refrigerate for 30 minutes.

04 Heat the grill to medium-high. After the fish have marinated, grill them for 3 to 4 minutes per side, uncovered, or until well charred and cooked through.

05 Transfer to a serving platter and spoon the dressing on top. Sprinkle with the coarse sea salt.

 To gut the sardines: First, cut off the head right above the gills, then slice the length of the belly. Use your thumb to remove the guts and discard. If you'd rather leave the head intact for presentation purposes, you can, but it will take a bit more effort to get the guts out. If you don't want anything to do with any of this, ask your fishmonger to do it for you. Keep in mind that the size of sardines varies greatly depending on the season.

brazilian fish stew

prep time: **10 minutes, plus 30 minutes to marinate** | cook time: **30 minutes** | serves: **4 to 6**

This stew has one of my favorite flavor profiles. I was blown away the first time I tried the combination of coconut, tomatoes, and citrus. It's one of those combinations that you just can't imagine until you try it, equally exotic and comforting.

▶ Make sure you: zest the lemon and lime before juicing them!

1 teaspoon finely grated lime zest, divided

1 teaspoon finely grated lemon zest, divided

¼ cup lime juice

¼ cup lemon juice

¼ cup chopped fresh cilantro, divided

1 pound wild cod, snapper, or any firm-fleshed, mild white fish fillets

1 pound large shrimp, peeled and deveined

1 tablespoon coconut oil

1 large onion, sliced

2 cloves garlic, minced

1 (14-ounce) jar diced tomatoes, with their juices

1 (14-ounce) can full-fat coconut milk

1½ teaspoons fish sauce

¼ to ½ teaspoon cayenne pepper

01 In a large, nonreactive bowl, combine ½ teaspoon of the lime zest, ½ teaspoon of the lemon zest, the lime and lemon juice, and 2 tablespoons of the chopped cilantro. Add the fish and shrimp and refrigerate, covered, for 30 minutes.

02 Melt the coconut oil in a medium soup pot over medium heat. Add the onion and sauté for 10 minutes, or until translucent. Add the garlic and sauté for 30 seconds more.

03 Add the tomatoes, coconut milk, fish sauce, and cayenne pepper. Simmer for 10 minutes, covered.

04 Add the fish and shrimp along with the marinade. Bring to a simmer and cook another 6 to 8 minutes, or until the fish starts to flake and the shrimp is cooked through.

05 Serve garnished with the remaining cilantro and citrus zest.

puttanesca fish en papillote

prep time: **30 minutes** | cook time: **12 minutes** | serves: **4**

Cooking fish in a parchment paper envelope will not only impress your friends, it is also a great way to impart tons of flavor in a short amount of time. If the idea of making these little bundles intimidates you, fear not: it's much easier than you think! See the step-by-step instructions on page 38.

▸ Make sure you have: parchment paper

▸ Make sure you: carefully cut open the parchment after cooking. Steam burns are no fun!

1 roma tomato, cut into small dice

8 Kalamata olives, pitted and minced

2 tablespoons capers, rinsed and drained

1 tablespoon minced fresh parsley

1 teaspoon minced anchovies (about 2 anchovies) or anchovy paste

½ teaspoon red pepper flakes

4 (6-ounce) pieces wild cod, halibut, snapper, or other mild white fish fillets

½ teaspoon finely ground sea salt

pinch of ground black pepper

1 lemon, sliced thin

1 tablespoon white wine, Chicken Broth (page 128), or lemon juice

01 Preheat the oven to 400°F.

02 Prepare four parchment hearts, following the instructions on page 38.

03 In a small bowl, combine the tomato, olives, capers, parsley, anchovies, and red pepper flakes.

04 Season the fish with the salt and pepper.

05 Onto each parchment heart, place 2 to 3 slices of lemon, then the fish, and then a heaping tablespoon of the tomato mixture. Pour ¾ teaspoon of wine onto each one.

06 Wrap them up as described on page 40.

07 Place the bundles on a rimmed baking sheet and bake for 10 minutes. Allow to rest 1 to 2 minutes. Serve the fish in the packets, cutting them open with kitchen shears just before serving.

smoky roast salmon with cucumber tomatillo salsa

prep time: **15 minutes** | cook time: **10 minutes** | serves: **4**

Super bright and fresh, tomatillo salsa is just the thing to spoon on top of smoky salmon for just the slightest kick. The flavors in this dish are more than you'd expect from something that can be on the table in less than 30 minutes.

finely grated zest of 1 lime

2 cloves garlic, minced

1 teaspoon ground cumin

1 teaspoon ground coriander

¼ teaspoon chipotle powder

1 teaspoon finely ground sea salt

2 tablespoons light olive oil

1½ pounds salmon fillets

thin lemon slices, for garnish (optional)

For the salsa

5 tomatillos, husked and rinsed

1 small cucumber, roughly chopped

1 small bunch fresh cilantro, roughly chopped

4 to 5 scallions, roughly chopped

1 jalapeño pepper, seeds and membrane removed, chopped

01 Preheat the oven to 425°F.

02 In a small bowl, combine the lime zest, garlic, spices, salt, and olive oil and rub on the salmon.

03 Roast the salmon for 5 to 8 minutes, depending on the thickness and fattiness, and then broil for 2 minutes.

04 Meanwhile, make the salsa: Pulse the tomatillos, cucumber, cilantro, scallions, and jalapeño in a food processor 6 to 8 times, or until it is the consistency of a smooth salsa.

05 Pour the salsa over the salmon, garnish with lemon slices, if using, and serve.

cilantro-lime roasted shrimp

prep time: **5 minutes, plus 30 minutes to marinate** | cook time: **5 minutes** | serves: **4**

Brining shrimp might seem unusual, but it's the simplest way to make good shrimp great. A quick soak in salt water infuses them with just the right salinity and gives them that great snap that we all know and love. Follow it with a quick roast and toss with a bright citrus dressing, and you've got yourself a super simple and delicious meal. These shrimp are excellent served hot with Coconut Cauli-Rice (page 223) or as a filling for Plantain Tortillas (page 246), or chilled and dipped in Rémoulade (page 58)—a great alternative to shrimp cocktail.

1½ pounds extra-large or jumbo shrimp (about 20 per pound), peeled and deveined

1 tablespoon coconut oil, melted

For the brine

2 tablespoons finely ground sea salt

1½ cups hot water

1 cup ice

For the dressing

1 tablespoon minced fresh cilantro

1 teaspoon ground coriander

1 tablespoon lime juice

pinch of cayenne pepper

pinch of garlic powder

1 tablespoon extra virgin olive oil

01 Make the brine: Dissolve the salt in the hot water, then stir in the ice.

02 Add the shrimp to the brine and refrigerate for 30 minutes.

03 Meanwhile, make the dressing: Combine the cilantro, coriander, lime juice, cayenne pepper, and garlic powder in a large bowl. Whisk in the olive oil.

04 Preheat the oven to 450°F and put a rimmed baking sheet in it to heat up.

05 Remove the shrimp from the brine and rinse under cold water.

06 Dry them well on paper towels and toss with the coconut oil.

07 Once the oven and baking sheet are hot, carefully place the shrimp onto the baking sheet in a single layer.

08 Roast for 2 minutes, carefully flip the shrimp, and roast for another 2 minutes.

09 Toss the shrimp in the dressing and serve either hot or chilled.

thai green curry mussels

prep time: **15 minutes** | cook time: **15 minutes** | serves: **4**

The proper way to eat mussels is by taking the shell of the first one you eat and using it to grab the rest, like little pinchers. The only problem with that method is that you don't get the sauce! Considering these mussels are simmered in a fragrant green curry coconut sauce infused with ginger, lemongrass, and chile, I recommend you slurp them right off the half shell. Sometimes you've just got to say, *to hell with proper.*

1 (2-inch) piece lemongrass from the bottom third of the stalk

2 tablespoons coconut oil

1 (1-inch) piece ginger, peeled and sliced thin

3 tablespoons green curry paste

2 Fresno or jalapeño peppers, sliced thin

1 cup Chicken Broth (page 128)

1½ cups full-fat coconut milk

2 pounds mussels, scrubbed and debearded (see Note)

¼ cup roughly chopped fresh cilantro, for garnish

01 Whack the lemongrass with the dull side of a chef's knife a few times, then slice it into 3 to 4 diagonal slices.

02 In a large sauté pan or wok, melt the coconut oil over medium heat.

03 Add the lemongrass and ginger. Sauté for 4 to 5 minutes, until fragrant.

04 Add the curry paste and Fresno peppers and sauté for another 30 seconds or so. Pour in the chicken broth and coconut milk. Bring to a boil and cook 1 minute.

05 Add the mussels and simmer for 5 minutes, or until all of the mussels open. Discard any that don't open. Garnish with the cilantro and serve.

 Note: Quite often, mussels are sold well cleaned and debearded. If that's not the case, give them a quick scrub under cold running water, and pull out the beards (the stringy piece between the shells) with your fingers or tweezers.

moules frites

prep time: **10 minutes** | cook time: **15 minutes** | serves: **4**

I can't say exactly why mussels and fries are the perfect pairing, but I know it to be true. For the full experience, make a batch of Mayonnaise (page 54) to dip your fries in.

2 cups duck fat, light olive oil, lard, or coconut oil, for frying

3 pounds russet potatoes (2 to 3 large potatoes), peeled and cut into ½-inch-wide sticks

1 cup finely diced shallots

2 tablespoons unsalted butter

1 tablespoon minced garlic (about 4 big cloves)

½ teaspoon finely ground sea salt, plus more for the fries

2 pounds mussels, scrubbed and debearded (see Note, page 152)

2 cups dry white wine

¼ cup minced fresh parsley

½ teaspoon minced fresh thyme leaves

1 cup Mayonnaise (page 54), for serving (optional)

01 In a medium saucepan, heat the fat or oil to 360°F. Fry the potatoes in 2 to 3 batches for about 5 minutes each, or until golden brown. Remove to a wire rack set over a rimmed baking sheet. Start the mussels once you're on your last batch of fries.

02 Sauté the shallots in the butter over medium-high heat for 3 to 4 minutes.

03 Add the garlic and sauté another 30 seconds. Add the salt and stir.

04 Add the mussels, shaking the pan for 30 seconds.

05 Turn the heat up to high and add the wine, parsley, and thyme.

06 Bring the liquid to a boil and cook for another 5 minutes, or until all of the mussels open. Discard any that remain closed.

07 Once all of the potatoes are fried, put them all back in the fat for 1 minute. Remove to a wire rack and shower with salt.

08 Serve the mussels and broth in shallow bowls with fries on the side. Serve with mayonnaise, if desired.

POULTRY AND RABBIT

perfect roast chicken

prep time: **5 minutes** | cook time: **1½ to 2 hours** | serves: **4**

Out of all the ways to roast a chicken, the simplest method is my favorite. The salt yields a crispy skin while keeping the meat inside moist.

▶ Make sure you have: a cast iron Dutch oven

1 whole chicken (3 to 4 pounds)

1 tablespoon finely ground sea salt

01 Preheat the oven to 425°F.

02 Coat the entire chicken with the salt and place in a Dutch oven, breast side up.

03 Roast the chicken, uncovered, for 1 hour 15 minutes, after which begin checking every 15 minutes until it's cooked through, reaching an internal temperature of 165°F.

04 Allow to rest for 10 to 15 minutes before carving.

citrus-herb spatchcock chicken

prep time: **15 minutes** | cook time: **55 minutes** | serves: **4**

Splitting a chicken down the middle—also called *spatchcocking*—is a great way to roast a whole bird in about half the time. It's easy to do, plus you'll have the backbone to use in your next batch of broth.

1 whole chicken (about 4 pounds)

2 lemons

2 small oranges

5 cloves garlic, smashed

1 teaspoon smoked paprika

1½ teaspoons finely ground sea salt

¼ teaspoon ground black pepper

1 small bunch fresh parsley, stems torn off and discarded

leaves from 2 sprigs fresh tarragon

01 Preheat the oven to 425°F.

02 To spatchcock the chicken: Place it breast side down on a cutting board, so you're looking at the backbone.

03 Using a sharp knife or poultry shears, cut along the right of the backbone from the tail end to the neck.

04 Repeat along the left side of the backbone.

05 Press down on the wings to flatten the bird and break the breastbone.

06 Flip the chicken over so the breast side is up.

07 Squeeze the juice of 1 lemon and 1 orange into a blender and add the garlic, paprika, salt, pepper, parsley, and tarragon. Puree until smooth.

08 Slice the remaining lemon and orange thinly and layer in the bottom of a roasting pan.

09 Rub the chicken all over with the marinade.

10 Place the chicken, breast side up, on the citrus slices in the roasting pan and roast for 45 minutes, or until the internal temperature reaches 165°F.

11 Allow to rest, loosely covered with aluminum foil, for 10 minutes before carving.

pan-roasted chicken with bacon and apples

prep time: **10 minutes** | cook time: **40 minutes** | serves: **4**

The bistro I used to work at in upstate New York served a dish called French Country Chicken in the fall. I've been making a version of that dish ever since, and it's always been one of my favorites. This method, searing the skin and then braising, yields tender meat while the skin stays crispy.

1 whole chicken, cut up into 8 pieces (see page 34)

1 teaspoon finely ground sea salt

¼ teaspoon ground black pepper

1 cup white wine

3 to 4 sprigs fresh thyme

½ pound bacon (5 to 6 thick strips)

1 cup sliced shallots (3 to 4 large)

1 apple, cored and sliced in ½-inch-thick half-moons

01 Preheat the oven to 450°F.

02 Season the chicken pieces liberally on both sides with the salt, and just on the flesh side with the pepper.

03 Heat a large, dry cast iron skillet (or other oven-safe skillet) over medium-high heat. Sear the chicken pieces skin side down in the hot skillet until nicely browned and crispy, about 4 to 5 minutes. Flip and cook on the flesh side for 2 minutes. Pour in the wine and nestle in the thyme sprigs. Roast in the oven for 15 minutes.

04 Meanwhile, brown the bacon in a medium skillet over medium heat until crisp, about 10 minutes.

05 Pour off all but about a tablespoon of the bacon fat and add the shallots and apple. Sauté for another 4 to 5 minutes, until the shallots are softened and the apple slices start to brown.

06 After the chicken has cooked for 15 minutes, add the bacon apple mixture to the pan with the chicken, doing your best to nestle it between the pieces as opposed to covering the skin.

07 Roast for another 10 to 15 minutes, or until the internal temperature of the chicken reaches 165°F.

crispy breaded
cinnamon chicken fingers

prep time: **20 minutes** | cook time: **20 minutes** | serves: **4 to 6**

Oh the elusive Paleo breading. Getting the flavor right isn't all that tricky, but getting it to stay on the meat? That's another story. Well, I'm happy to report that I've cracked the code. To celebrate this accomplishment, I've styled this recipe after one of my favorite dishes from my mom's kitchen. For years, anytime I was heading back to Connecticut to visit my family, my mom would ask what I wanted for dinner, and her oven-fried chicken was always the answer. Her version was made using a whole cut-up chicken, which was pan-fried and finished in the oven. But it seems like such a kid-friendly dish that I couldn't resist making it chicken finger–style with fast-cooking strips of boneless chicken.

1½ pounds boneless, skinless chicken thighs

¾ cup tapioca starch or arrowroot powder

2 teaspoons finely ground sea salt, divided

1 teaspoon ground black pepper, divided

3 large eggs, well beaten

2 cups almond meal

½ cup sesame seeds

1 teaspoon ground cumin

1 teaspoon ground coriander

1 teaspoon paprika

1 teaspoon ground cinnamon

⅔ cup duck fat, light olive oil, coconut oil, or lard

01 Pound the chicken thighs between two sheets of plastic wrap until they are ¼ inch thick. Cut into 1-inch-wide strips.

02 Set up your breading station: Set out 3 shallow bowls or small baking dishes.

03 In the first bowl, mix together the tapioca starch, ½ teaspoon of the salt, and ½ teaspoon of the pepper.

04 In the second bowl, beat the eggs.

05 In the third bowl, mix together the almond meal, sesame seeds, remaining 1½ teaspoons of the salt, remaining ½ teaspoon of the pepper, cumin, coriander, paprika, and cinnamon.

06 Dredge the chicken in the tapioca mixture, then in the eggs, then in the almond meal mixture.

07 Once all of the chicken is breaded, heat a large skillet over medium-high heat and pour in the fat. Heat to 360°F.

08 Fry the chicken for 1½ to 2 minutes per side. Remove to a wire rack set over a rimmed baking sheet. It should be cooked through at this point, but if it's on the thicker side and it's not, pop it in a 375°F oven for 5 minutes or so.

roasted rabbit
with grapes and pancetta

prep time: **15 minutes** | cook time: **30 minutes** | serves: **4**

Rabbit is such a lean meat that it loves to be cooked with something high in fat, such as pancetta. You can, of course, make this dish any time of year, but with the simplicity of the ingredients, I recommend trying it when grapes are in season and at their best.

3 ounces pancetta, cut into ½-inch strips

2 cloves garlic, minced

1 teaspoon minced fresh tarragon leaves (about 2 sprigs)

1 tablespoon minced fresh chervil (about 5 sprigs) or parsley

1 teaspoon Dijon mustard

¼ teaspoon finely ground sea salt

⅛ teaspoon ground black pepper

1 rabbit, cut into 6 pieces

½ pound red seedless grapes

01 Preheat the oven to 450°F.

02 Place a large, oven-safe skillet (large enough to fit the rabbit) over medium heat. Sauté the pancetta, stirring often, for 5 minutes, or until crisp. Drain on paper towels and set aside. Pour 2 tablespoons of the pancetta fat into a small bowl. (If there is less than 2 tablespoons, add some olive oil to make up the difference. If there is more, discard the rest or save it for future use.) Do not wash the skillet—you will be using it for the rabbit.

03 To the bowl with the fat, add the garlic, tarragon, chervil, mustard, salt, and pepper. Stir to combine.

04 Rub the rabbit with the herb-mustard mixture.

05 Place the rabbit and the grapes in the skillet you cooked the pancetta in. Roast in the oven for 20 minutes.

06 Sprinkle the rabbit with the reserved pancetta and bake another 5 minutes.

 Make-ahead tip: The pancetta can be cooked and the rabbit pieces coated in the herb-mustard mixture the day ahead. The day of, roast the rabbit with the grapes, following the instructions.

crispy braised duck legs with melted shallots and roasted plums

prep time: **15 minutes** | cook time: **2½ hours** | serves: **2 to 4**

It's beyond me why duck breast gets all the credit. If you ask me, it's the legs that deserve it. While I won't ever turn down a beautifully prepared, crispy-skinned duck breast, I'd much rather cook the legs, which boast super crispy skin and succulent, fall-off-the-bone tender meat. These gams are braised in Pinot Noir and served with roasted plums, and they're even better when made the day before.

1 teaspoon finely ground sea salt, divided

4 whole duck legs (about 2 pounds total)

1 pound shallots (about 5 to 6 large), cut into large dice

½ teaspoon ground black pepper

1½ cups dry red wine, such as Pinot Noir

1 cup Chicken Broth (page 128)

5 to 6 sprigs fresh thyme

1 pound plums (about 4 large), quartered

2 teaspoons honey (optional)

01 Preheat the oven to 300°F.

02 Salt the duck legs with about ½ teaspoon salt total on both sides. Heat a Dutch oven over medium-high heat. Once hot, add the duck legs, skin side down. Sear undisturbed for 5 to 7 minutes, or until the skin is brown and crispy. It should release easily from the bottom of the pan.

03 Flip the legs and sear on the flesh side for 2 to 3 minutes, and then remove to a plate.

04 Drain all but 1 tablespoon of the duck fat from the pan (reserve the rest for later use) and add the shallots. Sauté until golden, 2 to 3 minutes. Add the remaining ½ teaspoon of salt and the pepper. Turn the heat up to high and add the wine and chicken broth, scraping up any bits that are stuck to the pan. Add the thyme sprigs and bring to a boil. Once it's rolling, boil for 1 full minute.

05 Turn off the heat and add the duck legs back in, along with any juice that they released. Arrange them skin side up, with the flesh submerged in the liquid and the skin above the surface.

06 Cut a piece of parchment in a circle about the size of your pot and snug it in over the duck legs. Cover the pot and place in the oven.

07 Braise for 2 hours, then remove the pot from the oven and uncover, being careful of escaping steam. Remove the parchment and discard.

08 Turn the oven up to 475°F. Toss the plums with 1 tablespoon of the reserved duck fat and the honey, if using. Remove the duck legs from the braising liquid and place on a rimmed baking sheet, along with the plums.

09 Put the duck and plums in the hot oven and roast for 15 minutes, or until the plums are starting to soften and the duck skin is crispy.

10 Set the pot with the braising liquid over high heat and reduce until syrupy, about 5 minutes.

11 To serve, spoon the sauce onto a platter or individual plates, place the duck legs on top, and arrange the plums alongside.

 Make-ahead tip: Braise the duck legs up to 4 days ahead, saving the final roasting with the plums until right before serving.

whole roast duck with root vegetables and wild mushrooms

prep time: **30 minutes, including time to rehydrate the mushrooms** | cook time: **2 hours** | serves: **4**

Rich and fatty duck loves to be paired with earthy vegetables, and earthy vegetables just love to be cooked in duck fat. I think it's safe to say that this recipe is a great example of killing two birds (ducks!) with one stone.

1 ounce dried porcini or other wild mushrooms

1 whole duck (about 3 to 4 pounds)

1 lemon, halved

2 teaspoons finely ground sea salt, divided

3 sprigs fresh rosemary

3 carrots (about ½ pound), peeled or scrubbed and cut into large dice

3 large shallots, cut into large dice

2 parsnips (about ½ pound), cut into large dice

01 Preheat the oven to 325°F.

02 Soak the mushrooms in 1 cup of hot water for 30 minutes.

03 Place the duck breast side up in a roasting pan and squeeze ½ of the lemon over it. Sprinkle with 1 teaspoon of the salt.

04 Place both halves of the lemon and the rosemary inside the cavity of the duck.

05 Scatter the diced veggies around the duck in the pan and sprinkle with the remaining teaspoon of salt.

06 Add the reconstituted mushrooms, along with ½ cup of the liquid they soaked in, to the pan. (Slowly pour off the mushroom liquid, in case there is some dirt that has settled to the bottom.)

07 Roast in the oven for 30 minutes. Flip the bird and roast another 30 minutes. Flip it one more time, so the breast side is up, and roast 30 minutes more. Turn the heat up to 450°F and cook another 10 minutes to brown the skin.

08 Allow to rest, loosely covered with aluminum foil, for 15 to 20 minutes before carving.

09 Serve with the roasted veggies.

grilled lemon-ginger chicken

prep time: **10 minutes, plus 30 minutes to 2 hours to marinate** | cook time: **35 minutes** | serves: **4**

The super lemony marinade for this chicken penetrates quickly, making it a great weeknight supper. I love it grilled, but roasting it in the oven yields great results, too.

1 lemon, peeled and quartered

1 (1-inch) piece ginger, peeled and grated

¼ cup water or Chicken Broth (page 128)

3 cloves garlic, minced

1 teaspoon ground turmeric

1 teaspoon dry mustard

1 tablespoon light olive oil

pinch of saffron (optional)

1 whole chicken (3 to 4 pounds), cut up (see page 34)

01 In a blender, combine the lemon, ginger, water, garlic, turmeric, mustard, olive oil, and saffron, if using. Blend until smooth.

02 Cut a few slits into the meat of the breasts and thighs, about ½ inch deep. Place the chicken in a nonreactive container and coat it with the marinade, rubbing it all over and into the slits. Marinate it for at least 30 minutes and up to 2 hours, but not much longer.

03 Preheat the grill to medium-low. Grill the chicken with the lid closed for 30 to 35 minutes, or until the internal temperature reaches 165°F, flipping every 6 to 8 minutes. Adjust your grill as needed; they all run a little different.

04 Alternatively, to roast: Preheat the oven to 475°F. Roast the chicken for 30 to 35 minutes on a rimmed baking sheet, or until the internal temperature reaches 165°F.

MEAT

lamb curry

prep time: **15 minutes** | cook time: **2 to 2½ hours** | serves: **4**

Few things are as warming to the core as a bowl of spicy lamb curry. Serve this over Coconut Cauli-Rice (page 223) with Raita (page 66) on the side.

1 tablespoon minced garlic (4 to 6 cloves)

1 tablespoon peeled and grated ginger (about 2 inches)

1 tablespoon garam masala

2 teaspoons ground coriander

1 teaspoon ground turmeric

½ teaspoon cayenne pepper

½ teaspoon ground cardamom

1 teaspoon finely ground sea salt

1 tablespoon ghee or coconut oil

2 pounds lamb stew meat

2 medium onions, sliced

4 cups chopped tomatoes (about 2 large)

4 cardamom pods

6 whole cloves

2 small sweet potatoes, peeled and cut into medium dice

fresh mint leaves, for garnish (optional)

01 Combine the garlic, ginger, garam masala, coriander, turmeric, cayenne pepper, cardamom, and salt in a small bowl.

02 Heat a Dutch oven or medium stockpot over medium-high heat. Melt the ghee or coconut oil and sear the lamb on all sides, in batches so it doesn't crowd the pan. Remove the lamb and set it aside.

03 Add the onions to the pot and turn the heat down to medium. Sauté for about 10 minutes, or until golden brown and softened.

04 Add the garlic-ginger-spice mixture and sauté for 30 seconds, stirring constantly.

05 Add the tomatoes and their juice. Simmer for 5 minutes, adding a bit of water if needed so the spices don't burn.

06 Transfer half the tomato mixture to a blender and puree; alternately, coarsely puree with an immersion blender.

07 Return the sauce and lamb to the pot and add the whole cardamom pods and whole cloves. Turn the heat to low and simmer for 1 hour. Add the sweet potatoes and continue to cook for 30 to 45 minutes, or until the lamb and sweet potatoes are tender. Serve garnished with fresh mint leaves, if desired.

 Is your stovetop simmer-stubborn? Many of them are, burning too hot for the slow simmer we need for low-slow cooking. If you have a Dutch oven, I recommend cooking this in the oven, instead: 300°F for 1½ to 2 hours, adding the sweet potatoes about halfway through.

moroccan shepherd's pie

prep time: **15 minutes** | cook time: **1 hour 10 minutes** | serves: **4 to 6**

Shepherd's pie is classic, old-school comfort food, my favorite kind of dish to put a twist on. This version has more flavor than should fit in a casserole dish, without losing any of that stick-to-your-ribs feeling.

3 pounds yams (about 3 large), peeled and roughly chopped

2 tablespoons ghee or unsalted butter

2 teaspoons finely ground sea salt, divided

2 pounds ground lamb

1 large onion (1-plus pound), grated

2 carrots (½ pound), peeled or scrubbed and grated

1 parsnip (⅓ pound), peeled and grated

2 tablespoons tomato paste

1½ teaspoons ground cumin

2 teaspoons ground coriander

½ teaspoons ground cardamom

⅛ teaspoon ground cinnamon

⅛ teaspoon ground clove

⅛ teaspoon cayenne pepper

¼ teaspoon ground black pepper

1 cup Chicken Broth (page 128) or water

01 Preheat the oven to 425°F.

02 Boil the yams for 15 to 20 minutes, until tender. Drain and mash with a potato masher or put through a ricer. Mix in the ghee and ½ teaspoon of the salt.

03 In a large skillet over medium-high heat, brown the lamb. Remove to a bowl, leaving about a tablespoon of fat in the pan.

04 In the same skillet you cooked the lamb, sauté the onion, carrots, and parsnip over medium heat until soft, about 10 minutes. Add the tomato paste, spices, and remaining 1½ teaspoons of salt. Cook another minute, then add the broth. Return the lamb and stir to combine.

05 Transfer the lamb mixture to a medium baking dish and top with the mashed yams.

06 Bake for 25 to 30 minutes, until bubbling around the edges. Allow to rest 5 to 10 minutes before serving.

lamb stew with tomatoes, oranges, and olives

prep time: **10 minutes** | cook time: **2 hours** | serves: **4**

This recipe is based on my favorite Mario Batali recipe, which is made with boneless leg of lamb. The combination of the tomato, wine, oranges, and olives creates an incredible flavor that I find myself craving often. While it may seem counterintuitive to leave the oranges unpeeled, the rind adds a fantastic depth to the sauce, and they practically fall apart by the time the stew is done.

1 tablespoon ghee, lard, or unsalted butter

2 pounds lamb stew meat

1 large red onion, thinly sliced

3 cloves garlic, sliced

2 medium oranges, preferably blood oranges, cut into half-moons, peel on

5 sprigs fresh thyme

1 cup full-bodied red wine

1 cup jarred crushed tomatoes

1 cup Castelvetrano olives (big, green, mild ones)

1 batch Parsnip Puree (page 208) or Cauliflower Rice (page 222), for serving

01 Preheat the oven to 300°F.

02 Heat the fat in a Dutch oven over medium-high heat. Sear the lamb in the fat until brown on all sides. Work in two or more batches so you don't crowd the pan. Remove the browned lamb to a bowl to catch the juices.

03 Add the onion and sauté for 5 minutes, or until brown and softened.

04 Add the garlic, oranges, thyme, wine, tomatoes, and olives. Bring to a simmer, scraping up any brown bits on the bottom of the pan.

05 Simmer 2 minutes, then return the lamb to the pot and turn off the heat.

06 Cover the Dutch oven and braise in the oven for 1½ hours, or until the lamb is tender.

07 Serve over parsnip puree or cauliflower rice.

fresh herb lamb burgers with raita

prep time: **15 minutes** | cook time: **10 minutes** | serves: **4**

Bored of the same old burger? Why not switch it up a bit? These lamb burgers, served with cooling raita, are guaranteed to get you out of your burger slump.

1½ pounds ground lamb

¼ cup minced fresh parsley (about ¼ bunch)

2 tablespoons minced fresh mint leaves (about 5 sprigs)

15 to 20 fresh chives, minced

½ teaspoon finely ground sea salt

¼ teaspoon ground black pepper

1 tablespoon ghee or preferred fat

For serving

butter lettuce leaves, for wrapping

1 batch Raita (page 66)

cucumber slices

tomato slices

01 In a large bowl, mix the lamb, herbs, salt, and pepper together with your hands until well incorporated.

02 Form into 4 burgers.

03 Heat a large skillet or griddle over medium-high heat. Melt the ghee in the pan.

04 Pan-fry the burgers for 3 to 4 minutes on each side, or until cooked through.

05 Serve wrapped in butter lettuce leaves with raita and veggies.

 These are also excellent made into bite-sized meatballs and served as hors d'oeuvres. Bake in a 425°F oven for 15 to 20 minutes, or until golden brown and cooked through. Serve with Raita (page 66) for dipping.

pistachio-crusted rack of lamb

prep time: **10 minutes** | cook time: **25 minutes** | serves: **2**

Nine times out of ten, I simply salt and pepper rack of lamb and sear it. It's such a delicious cut of meat, it doesn't need much more than that. But for a special occasion, roasting it with a pistachio crust is just the thing to fancy it up. And it's still so simple to prepare, that special occasion could simply be . . . Tuesday night.

scant ½ teaspoon finely ground sea salt

⅛ teaspoon ground black pepper

1 rack of lamb (8 bones)

1 tablespoon ghee or light olive oil

For the crust

¼ cup shelled raw pistachios

10 leaves fresh mint

1 teaspoon minced garlic (about 3 cloves)

1 teaspoon peeled and minced fresh ginger (about ½ inch)

finely grated zest of 1 lemon

scant ¾ teaspoon finely ground sea salt

1 tablespoon melted ghee, unsalted butter, or light olive oil

01 Preheat the oven to 400°F.

02 Sprinkle the salt and pepper on the lamb.

03 Heat a skillet over medium-high heat and add the ghee.

04 Once it's shimmering, add the lamb, searing on each side for 3 minutes, or until you get a good crust. Remove to a baking dish that's just large enough to fit the lamb.

05 Make the crust: In a food processor, pulse the pistachios 7 or 8 times, until they're fine crumbs. Add the mint, garlic, ginger, lemon zest, and salt and pulse 2 to 3 more times, until incorporated. Pulse in the melted ghee.

06 Pack the pistachio mixture onto the lamb as best you can and roast for 15 to 20 minutes, or until done to your liking. For medium-rare, you want a temperature of 130°F.

07 Allow to rest for 5 minutes before slicing between the bones and serving.

pork chops with stone fruit slaw

prep time: **15 minutes** | cook time: **12 to 16 minutes** | serves: **4**

Summer's best stone fruit is only around for a short time, so I love using it while it's here. Make sure to get firm fruit that can be cut into matchsticks and isn't yet too sweet.

1 pound firm stone fruit (about 2 large and 2 small, any combination you'd like)

¼ teaspoon chili powder (or chipotle powder if you want it to have a kick)

1 teaspoon finely grated lime zest

1 teaspoon lime juice

1 teaspoon finely ground sea salt, divided

1 teaspoon ground cumin

1 teaspoon ground coriander

1 teaspoon paprika

4 bone-in pork chops, about 1 inch thick

1 tablespoon lard, coconut oil, or light olive oil

01 Julienne the stone fruit (see page 29 for julienne instructions). Place in a bowl with the chili powder, lime zest and juice, and a pinch of the salt.

02 In a small bowl, mix together the cumin, coriander, paprika, and remaining salt.

03 Season the pork chops on both sides with spice and salt mixture.

04 Heat a large skillet over medium-high heat and melt the lard. Sear the pork chops for 3 to 4 minutes per side, or until almost cooked through. Remove to a serving dish and cover loosely with foil, allowing it to rest for 5 minutes before serving with the stone fruit slaw.

pork chops with caramelized apples

prep time: **5 minutes** | cook time: **15 minutes** | serves: **4**

Pork chops and applesauce, all grown up.

1½ teaspoons finely ground sea salt

⅛ teaspoon ground black pepper

4 bone-in pork chops, about ¾ inch thick

2 tablespoons lard or preferred cooking oil, divided

3 apples, sliced into ¼-inch-thick wedges

¼ teaspoon ground cinnamon

¼ teaspoon ground cardamom

¼ teaspoon ground ginger

½ cup hard cider (see Note)

3 sprigs fresh thyme

01 Sprinkle the salt and pepper on the pork chops and allow the chops to come to room temperature. Heat a large skillet over medium-high heat and melt 1 tablespoon of the lard. Sear the pork chops for 3 to 4 minutes per side, or until almost cooked through. Remove to a serving dish and cover with foil.

02 Add the remaining tablespoon of the lard to the pan and add the apples. Shake the pan a few times, cooking the apples until they're golden on both sides, about 2 minutes. Add the spices and stir for 30 seconds.

03 Add the hard cider and thyme and bring to a simmer. Scrape the bottom of the pan to release any browned bits. Reduce for 3 minutes, or until the liquid is almost all gone.

04 Serve the apples and thickened sauce over the pork chops.

 Note: If you'd rather skip the booze, use ¼ cup apple juice, ¼ cup water, and 1 tablespoon white wine vinegar instead.

cocoa-chili pork shoulder

prep time: **10 minutes** | cook time: **3 to 4 hours** | serves: **4 with leftovers**

Anytime there's a good-sized pork shoulder at the farmers market on Sunday, I buy it. Even though it has a long cooking time, it basically cooks itself. Good pork doesn't need much as far as seasoning goes, and the subtle cocoa and chili spice is a great counterpoint to the fattiness of the pork.

1 teaspoon finely ground sea salt

1 teaspoon smoked paprika

1 teaspoon cocoa powder

1 teaspoon ground coriander

1 teaspoon dried oregano

⅛ teaspoon chipotle powder

⅛ teaspoon ground cinnamon

4 pounds pork shoulder

5 to 6 cloves garlic, peeled

1 lime, halved

small handful of fresh cilantro leaves, for garnish (optional)

01 Preheat the oven to 300°F.

02 In a small bowl, mix together the salt, smoked paprika, cocoa powder, coriander, oregano, chipotle powder, and cinnamon. Rub it all over the pork and place in a Dutch oven. Scatter the garlic cloves in the pot. Cover the pot and place in the oven.

03 Cook for 3 to 4 hours, or until fork-tender. Allow to cool slightly before pulling it apart with two forks. Squeeze with fresh lime juice before serving. Garnish with the cilantro leaves, if using.

ginger scallion pork meatballs

prep time: **10 minutes** | cook time: **20 minutes** | serves: **4 (about 30 small meatballs)**

These have been in the rotation on my catering menus for years and are always a client favorite. They're also extremely versatile: Make them bite-sized and serve them as hors d'oeuvres, drop them into chicken broth for wonton-less soup (they happen to taste just like the inside of a wonton), or serve them over Sesame Zucchini Noodles (page 212) for a simple and satisfying supper.

1 tablespoon lard or coconut oil, melted

3 tablespoons coconut aminos

2 teaspoons toasted sesame oil

1 tablespoon fish sauce

1 tablespoon coconut flour

1 small bunch scallions, minced (about 10 skinny)

1½ tablespoons peeled and grated fresh ginger

1½ pounds ground pork

01 Preheat the oven to 425°F. Lightly grease a rimmed baking sheet with the lard.

02 In a large bowl, mix together the coconut aminos, sesame oil, fish sauce, coconut flour, scallions, and ginger. Add the pork and mix with your hands until well combined.

03 Roll into golf ball–sized balls and place on the prepared baking sheet. Bake for 15 to 20 minutes, or until thoroughly cooked and golden.

 Variation: Ground chicken thigh meat works great in this recipe, too.

twice-cooked pork belly

prep time: **15 minutes** | cook time: **1 hour 15 minutes** | serves: **4**

When I first heard of boiling pork belly as the first step in twice-cooking it, I was skeptical. I imagined boiled pork belly to be rubbery and bland. But in actuality, the boiling renders some of the extra fat, just enough to ensure it gets super crispy and tender when you stir-fry it.

2 pounds pork belly, skin removed

1 teaspoon finely ground sea salt

1 small head green cabbage, diced (about 2 cups)

1 tablespoon coconut oil

1 small leek, white and light green parts only, sliced

5 to 6 mini sweet bell peppers or 1 large bell pepper (red, orange, or yellow), sliced

1 teaspoon peeled and grated ginger

1 bunch scallions, cut into 1-inch lengths

2 tablespoons coconut aminos

2 tablespoons sherry

1 tablespoon fish sauce

½ teaspoon red pepper flakes

1 batch Cauliflower Rice (page 222) or Zucchini Noodles (page 210), for serving (optional)

01 Place the pork belly in a pot just big enough to fit it. Cover the belly with water. Remove the belly, add the salt, and bring to a boil.

02 Return the belly to the water once it's boiling and boil for 45 minutes to 1 hour, or until it is tender enough to be easily pierced with a sharp knife. Remove it from the water. Once it is cool enough to handle, slice thinly.

03 In a large skillet or wok, stir-fry the cabbage in the coconut oil for 5 minutes, or until softened. Add the leek and the peppers and stir-fry for another 2 to 3 minutes, or until softened. Remove to a bowl.

04 Add the pork to the pan and stir-fry for 4 minutes, turning often (in batches, if need be). Once it starts to get crispy, add the leek and peppers back in, along with the scallions, coconut aminos, sherry, fish sauce, and red pepper flakes. Stir-fry for 1 to 2 more minutes, or until the sauce is simmering and the scallions have wilted.

05 Serve over cauliflower rice or zucchini noodles, if desired.

seared steaks with pan sauce

prep time: **5 minutes** | cook time: **15 minutes** | serves: **4**

On plenty of occasions, I've heard people who have switched to a Paleo diet lament not having anything to put on their steak. People miss their steak sauce. Since good steak really doesn't need much, I wanted to create a sauce that was incredibly simple to make and elevated the flavor of the steak without drowning it. You'll be amazed at how much flavor can come out of three or so ingredients!

finely ground sea salt

4 (6- to 8-ounce) New York strip or rib-eye steaks, about 1 inch thick

1 tablespoon lard, melted or softened

3 tablespoons coconut aminos

3 tablespoons golden balsamic, white wine, or champagne vinegar

1 tablespoon Dijon mustard

a few sprigs of fresh herbs, such as rosemary, thyme, or oregano (optional)

01 Liberally salt the steaks and allow them to come to room temperature, about 30 minutes. Pat them dry and coat them lightly with the lard.

02 Heat a large, heavy-bottomed skillet over high heat.

03 Once the pan is very hot, add the steaks and sear for 3 to 4 minutes per side for medium-rare, or longer if you like more well-done steaks. Remove from the pan and allow to rest for 5 minutes, loosely covered with aluminum foil.

04 In a small bowl, mix together the coconut aminos, vinegar, and mustard. Allow the pan to cool a bit before adding the vinegar mixture and the herbs, if using, to the pan. Using the residual heat in the pan, reduce by about half, but do not turn it into a syrup. If that happens, simply add a bit of water to bring it back to a liquid.

05 After the steaks have rested, slice and serve with the sauce.

chili

prep time: **20 minutes** | cook time: **1 hour 20 minutes** | serves: **4 to 6**

In my pre-Paleo days, I used to eat around the beans as much as possible when I ate chili. I know that they're a traditional ingredient in many versions, but they never seemed right in there to me. What does seem right to me, when it comes to flavor, is lots of heat, balanced with just the right amount of smokiness and depth. And, of course, meat. If you don't eat pork, feel free to make this with all beef instead.

2 tablespoons lard or coconut oil, divided

1½ pounds ground beef

½ pound ground pork

1 large onion, cut into medium dice

2 bell peppers (red, orange, yellow, or a combination; about ¾ pound), cut into medium dice

5 cloves garlic, peeled and roughly chopped

1½ teaspoons finely ground sea salt

2 tablespoons chili powder

1 tablespoon ground coriander

1 tablespoon ground cumin

1 teaspoon paprika

⅛ teaspoon ground cinnamon

1 tablespoon cocoa powder

2 tablespoons tomato paste

1 cup brewed coffee (decaf is fine)

1 (28-ounce) jar diced tomatoes

2 to 3 tablespoons minced chipotle peppers or chipotle paste

01 Heat a Dutch oven over medium-high heat and add 1 tablespoon of the lard. Brown the meats for 4 to 5 minutes, in batches if necessary. Remove from the pan and set aside.

02 Add the remaining tablespoon of lard to the pan. Sauté the onion over medium-high heat for 5 minutes, stirring occasionally.

03 Add the peppers and garlic cloves and sauté for 3 more minutes, stirring occasionally, until the garlic is browned and the peppers have begun to soften.

04 Add the salt, spices, cocoa powder, and tomato paste and cook until the paste is brick red.

05 Add the coffee and reduce over medium-high heat until half the liquid is evaporated.

06 Return the meat to the pan and add the tomatoes and chipotle peppers.

07 Turn the heat to low and cover. Cook for 45 minutes over low heat, and then uncover and cook for another 15 minutes.

08 Serve with your favorite chili toppings.

coffee-rubbed flat iron fajitas

prep time: **10 minutes, plus 1 hour to marinate** | cook time: **25 minutes** | serves: **4**

There is a bit of work required to have a fajita party, but you can make the tortillas in advance if need be. They reheat wonderfully over a gas flame, on a grill, or in the oven. If you want to keep it even simpler, serve the steak and veggies with lettuce leaves instead.

1 pound flat iron steak

1 tablespoon lard or coconut oil

2 medium onions (red, white, or yellow, or a combination)

2 bell peppers (red, orange, yellow, or a combination), sliced

For the rub

1 teaspoon ground coffee

1 teaspoon chili powder

¾ teaspoon smoked paprika

¾ teaspoon coconut sugar

½ teaspoon ground coriander

½ teaspoon dried oregano

½ teaspoon ground black pepper

¼ teaspoon ground ginger

¼ teaspoon ground cumin

½ teaspoon finely ground sea salt

For serving

1 batch Plantain Tortillas (page 246)

1 batch Guacamole (page 48) or avocado slices

salsa of your choice

lime wedges

01 Combine the coffee, spices, and salt in a small bowl. Rub into the steak and set aside, for up to 1 hour.

02 Preheat the grill or grill pan to medium-high.

03 Heat a large skillet over medium-high heat. Melt the lard and sauté the onions for 4 to 5 minutes, until golden brown and beginning to soften. Add the peppers and sauté another 3 to 4 minutes, until crisp-tender. Set aside and keep warm.

04 Grill the steak for 3 to 4 minutes per side for medium-rare, or longer if you like your steak more well-done. Allow to rest for 5 minutes, loosely covered with aluminum foil, before cutting it against the grain into thin slices.

05 To serve: Push the onions and peppers to one side of the pan and place the sliced steak on the other side.

06 Serve with warm plantain tortillas, guacamole, your favorite salsa, and lime wedges.

 Tip: If you don't have a grill or grill pan, you can cook the meat in a cast iron skillet instead.

orange-ginger beef stir-fry

prep time: **10 minutes, plus 30 minutes to 2 hours to marinate** | cook time: **10 minutes** | serves: **4**

Some of my favorite meals are ones where the marinade becomes the sauce. Normally marinades are tossed out since they've had raw meat in them. That's a shame, because they're incredibly flavorful. All they need is some time over the heat; when cooked long enough, they are perfectly safe to eat.

1¼ pounds sirloin

1 batch Stir-Fry Marinade and Sauce (page 60)

1 tablespoon arrowroot powder

2 tablespoons coconut oil, divided

wide strips of orange zest (reserved from preparing the marinade and sauce)

½ pound string beans, stemmed and cut in half crosswise

1 jalapeño pepper, thinly sliced (seeded for a milder version)

½ pound bok choy, chopped

2 teaspoons black and/or white sesame seeds, for garnish

1 batch Cauliflower Rice (page 222) or Zucchini Noodles (page 210), for serving (optional)

01 Cut the beef across the grain into thin slices and place in a bowl with the stir-fry sauce. Marinate for 30 minutes, or up to 2 hours. Set aside. (It's fine to leave it at room temperature for up to 1 hour, but refrigerate if you'll be marinating it longer.)

02 Remove the beef from the sauce and drain well, reserving the liquid.

03 Stir the arrowroot into the reserved liquid.

04 Heat 1 tablespoon of the oil in a large skillet or wok over medium heat. Add the orange zest and cook for 2 minutes, or until brown on the edges.

05 Turn the heat to high, add the beef to the skillet or wok, and stir-fry for 2 minutes, or until brown on both sides. Remove the beef and the orange peels to the bowl with the sauce.

06 Wipe out the pan, add the remaining tablespoon of coconut oil, and place over medium-high heat. When the oil is melted and glistening, add the string beans and the jalapeño. Stir-fry for 3 to 4 minutes; you want the string beans to blister a bit.

07 Put the beef, orange zest, bok choy, and sauce in the pan and cook for another minute or two, until the sauce boils and thickens a bit and the bok choy wilts.

08 Sprinkle with the sesame seeds and serve over cauliflower rice or zucchini noodles, if desired.

VEGGIES AND SIDES

cumin-orange roasted carrots

prep time: **5 minutes** | cook time: **12 to 14 minutes** | serves: **4**

While I've never been a fan of the sweet glazed variety, I do love roasted carrots as a side dish. The combination of cumin and orange here is just enough to elevate the simple carrot to a level of understated sophistication.

1 pound carrots, peeled or scrubbed and cut into ½-inch-by-4-inch sticks

1 tablespoon unsalted butter, melted

1 teaspoon ground cumin

¼ teaspoon sumac (optional)

¼ teaspoon finely ground sea salt

finely grated zest of 1 small orange or clementine

1 tablespoon orange or clementine juice

pinch of coarse sea salt

01 Place the carrots on a rimmed baking sheet and toss with the butter, cumin, sumac, if using, and ¼ teaspoon of salt.

02 Roast 12 to 14 minutes, until crisp-tender.

03 Toss with the zest and orange juice.

04 Sprinkle with the coarse sea salt.

 If you don't have sumac on hand, this recipe is still great without it.

parsnip puree

prep time: **15 minutes** | cook time: **35 to 45 minutes** | serves: **4 to 6**

Oh the humble parsnip, so underrated. Poor thing must have an inferiority complex sitting next to the almighty carrot day after day in the produce aisle. Most people don't think to cook with it, and even when they do, it's most often tossed into stocks, not actually eaten. Let's fix that. Parsnips are delicious, after all, especially when roasted and then whipped until silky smooth. This recipe can be made thick, like mashed potatoes, or turned into an elegant puree.

2 pounds parsnips, peeled and cut into large dice

½ teaspoon finely ground sea salt

¼ teaspoon ground black pepper

pinch of ground nutmeg

2 tablespoons duck fat or unsalted butter, melted

1½ to 2 cups Chicken Broth (page 128), warmed

3 tablespoons unsalted butter or ghee

1 tablespoon Dijon mustard

01 Preheat the oven to 425°F.

02 In a bowl, toss the parsnips with the salt, pepper, nutmeg, and melted duck fat. Spread on a rimmed baking sheet.

03 Roast for 35 to 45 minutes, until very soft, shaking the pan after 20 minutes or so.

04 Transfer the roasted parsnips to a food processor and blend, adding 1½ cups of the chicken broth through the chute to incorporate. Add the butter and mustard. Add up to ½ cup more chicken broth if a silky smooth puree is desired, less if you want it closer to the consistency of mashed potatoes.

zucchini noodles

prep time: **30 minutes** | cook time: **0 to 5 minutes** | serves: **4**

Zucchini noodles, otherwise known as *zoodles*, are the classic Paleo pasta stand-in. You can use them in just about any dish that traditionally has pasta. Bonus: you get the pasta experience, but you're actually eating a vegetable. My carb-loving stepdaughter even deemed these "better than normal pasta."

2 pounds zucchini (6 to 7 medium)

1 teaspoon finely ground sea salt

01 Peel the zucchini, if desired. (This is completely optional, but it's sometimes a good idea if you're trying to replicate the look of spaghetti.)

02 With either a julienne peeler or a spiral slicer, julienne the zucchini into long, spaghetti-like strands.

03 Toss them with the salt in a colander and allow to sit for 20 to 30 minutes.

04 Give them a good rinse with cold water and drain.

05 To further dry them, lay on several layers of paper towels or a clean tea towel.

06 Depending on the dish you're serving them with, you can leave them raw and heat them in the sauce you'll be eating them with, toss them into a dry skillet to heat through and soften, or simply toss them with sauce to serve them at room temperature.

sesame zucchini noodles

prep time: **30 minutes** | serves: **4**

Anytime my dad had to bring a dish to a potluck, Szechuan peanut noodles were his stand-by. And for good reason, too. They were spicy, garlicky, intensely flavorful, and great at room temperature. For my take on them, I've subbed zucchini noodles, made them gingery instead of garlicky, and of course used tahini instead of peanut butter. Even with all of the changes I made, though, these are still quite reminiscent of his signature dish.

2 pounds zucchini (about 6-7 medium)

1 teaspoon finely ground sea salt

¼ cup tahini

1 (1-inch) piece fresh ginger, peeled and grated

2 tablespoons coconut aminos

1 tablespoon toasted sesame oil

1 teaspoon fish sauce

½ teaspoon red pepper flakes

2 tablespoons black and/or white sesame seeds, for garnish (optional)

1 small bunch scallions, sliced, for garnish (optional)

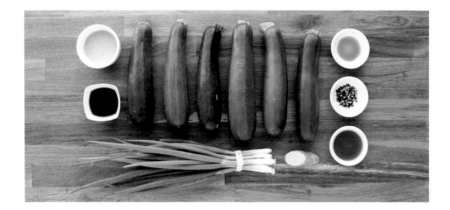

01 Peel the zucchini (if desired) and julienne with either a julienne peeler or spiral slicer.

02 Place in a colander and toss with the salt. Allow to sit and sweat out the excess liquid for 20 to 30 minutes.

03 Meanwhile, mix together the tahini, grated ginger, coconut aminos, sesame oil, fish sauce, and red pepper flakes.

04 Once the zucchini noodles have sat for 20 to 30 minutes, give them a rinse under cold water and drain them well. Dump them out onto several layers of paper towels or a kitchen towel to get out any excess moisture.

05 Stir the noodles into the sauce and top with sesame seeds and sliced scallions, if desired.

 Are you a big-time garlic lover? Feel free to mince a clove and add it to the sesame sauce.

spaghetti squash carbonara

prep time: **10 minutes** | cook time: **50 minutes** | serves: **4**

True carbonara is simplicity at its finest. While I recommend using the finest ingredients available in all recipes, I absolutely insist with this one. My favorite way to serve this dish is with the egg yolk nested on top of the "pasta," so that each guest can stir it in and create a creamy sauce. The heat of the squash will cook the yolk a bit, but if you'd rather not serve semi-raw egg yolks, follow the alternate instructions at the end of this recipe. Since this dish is more starch than protein, I put it in the veggies category, but it could easily take center stage as a main course.

▶ Cheesy recipe alert! This recipe has dairy and doesn't offer a substitution. If you eat cheese, proceed and enjoy. If not, avert your eyes.

1 small spaghetti squash (about 2½ pounds)

1 tablespoon light olive oil, melted bacon fat, or preferred fat

½ teaspoon finely ground sea salt

¼ teaspoon ground black pepper

2 egg whites

1 cup freshly grated Parmesan cheese (about 3 ounces)

¾ pound bacon, cut into lardons (¼-inch strips)

4 egg yolks

thinly sliced fresh chives, for garnish (optional)

01 Preheat the oven to 375°F and line a rimmed baking sheet with parchment paper.

02 Carefully cut the squash in half lengthwise and scoop out the seeds. Brush the cut-side with the olive oil and sprinkle with the salt and pepper. Place cut side up in a baking dish.

03 Roast for 30 to 40 minutes, until soft but not mushy. Once it's cooled enough to handle, use a fork to remove the squash strands from the skin. (You should have 4 cups cooked squash.)

04 Whisk together the 2 egg whites and Parmesan in a medium bowl.

05 Heat a large skillet over medium heat and cook the bacon until it's crispy. Remove with a slotted spoon, leaving 2 tablespoons fat in the pan. (Reserve the rest for future use.)

06 Add the cooked spaghetti squash to the pan with the bacon fat and cook over medium heat for 2 to 3 minutes.

07 Remove from the heat and slowly pour in the egg whites and Parmesan mixture, stirring constantly. Stir in the bacon, reserving a small amount for garnish.

08 Divide the spaghetti squash among four pasta bowls. Make a small nest in the top of each and place an egg yolk on top. Garnish with the reserved bacon and chives, if using.

Alternate instructions: If you prefer to cook the egg yolks a bit more, stir the yolks into the egg white–Parmesan mixture. Continue with the recipe as written, still taking the pasta off the heat before mixing in the egg and Parmesan mixture.

roasted sunchokes with rosemary salt

prep time: **10 minutes** | cook time: **25 minutes** | serves: **4**

You know how there are samples people in grocery stores, handing out little cups of granola, green juice, and gluten-free pasta? (Can you guess where I shop?) The sunchoke, or Jerusalem artichoke, needs some samples people. I'm willing to bet that they get passed by simply because most people have no idea what lurks inside. When roasted, they are creamier than a potato will ever be, and the skins roast up nicely, creating a fabulous bit of crunch. I like to keep them simple, with just a shower of rosemary salt, to let their interesting, nutty flavor come through.

1 pound sunchokes (Jerusalem artichokes), cut into large dice, peel on

2 tablespoons unsalted butter, duck fat, or fat of choice, melted

¼ teaspoon finely ground sea salt

2 teaspoons minced fresh rosemary

¼ teaspoon coarse sea salt

⅛ teaspoon ground black pepper

01 Preheat the oven to 475°F.

02 In a large bowl, toss the sunchokes with the melted butter and finely ground sea salt.

03 Transfer to a rimmed baking sheet and roast for 20 to 25 minutes, until soft and golden.

04 Meanwhile, combine the rosemary with the coarse sea salt and black pepper in a small bowl.

05 Sprinkle the roasted sunchokes with the rosemary salt and serve.

roasted asparagus

prep time: **5 minutes** | cook time: **10 to 20 minutes** | serves: **4**

Doesn't it seem as if asparagus season is over as soon as it starts? Such a shame, considering asparagus just might be the simplest veggie to cook! I get as much asparagus as I possibly can in early spring when it starts popping up at the farmers market, and roasting it is by far my favorite method. Roasted asparagus is excellent simply sprinkled with salt and pepper, but it's also great tossed with a vinaigrette, drizzled with hollandaise, or dipped in aioli.

1 pound asparagus (medium thickness or more recommended for this technique)

2 tablespoons light olive oil, melted duck fat, or fat of choice

½ teaspoon finely ground sea salt

¼ teaspoon ground black pepper

For serving (optional)

Champagne Vinaigrette (page 53), Lemony Hollandaise Sauce (page 62), a squeeze of lemon juice and a sprinkle of zest, or an aioli of your choice (page 56)

01 Preheat the oven to 375°F.

02 To trim the asparagus: Hold a single spear between your thumb and forefinger, towards the bottom of the spear. Bend it and it will snap in the exact spot that the woody end meets the juicy stalk. Once one spear is trimmed, you can line it up with the rest, and trim them in the same spot as the one you snapped.

03 Toss the asparagus with the oil and place on a rimmed baking sheet.

04 Roast for 10 to 20 minutes, depending on thickness. The spears should be golden brown and softened but not mushy.

05 Sprinkle with the salt and pepper and serve with vinaigrette, hollandaise, lemon juice and zest, or aioli, if desired.

best brussels

prep time: **10 minutes** | cook time: **30 minutes** | serves: **4**

I'm guilty of getting into a loop when it comes to Brussels sprouts: Roast 'em, shower 'em with truffle salt, eat, repeat. Not that there's anything wrong with that, but I'm a big fan of mixing it up a little. For this recipe I decided to go way outside of my truffled Brussels comfort zone. I was surprised at how good they came out, and I'm pretty sure I've found myself a new loop to get into.

1 pound Brussels sprouts, ends cut off and halved

1 tablespoon melted duck fat

2 tablespoons fish sauce

2 teaspoons coconut sugar

1 teaspoon peeled and grated ginger

1 Fresno or jalapeño pepper, minced

1 tablespoon lime juice

01 Preheat the oven to 425°F. Place one oven rack in the center and another at the highest position.

02 In a large bowl, toss together the Brussels sprouts and duck fat to coat well. Transfer to a rimmed baking sheet and roast for 25 minutes.

03 In the same bowl used for the Brussels sprouts, mix together the fish sauce, coconut sugar, ginger, and Fresno pepper.

04 After roasting for 25 minutes, add the Brussels sprouts to the bowl with the fish sauce mixture and toss to coat. Return to the baking sheet and turn the broiler to high.

05 Return to the oven and broil the Brussels sprouts for 3 to 4 minutes, and then toss them with the lime juice. Serve hot.

cauliflower rice

prep time: **5 minutes** | cook time: **5 minutes** | serves: **4**

I'll admit that the first time I saw a recipe for cauliflower rice, I was skeptical. After all, cauliflower tastes like cauliflower, not like rice. After making it once, though, I was a believer. The texture was so much closer than I thought it would be, and when cooked with the right amount of fat and salt, it's the perfect stand-in for the grain it's mimicking.

1 large head cauliflower (about 2 pounds)

2 tablespoons unsalted butter, coconut oil, or preferred fat

½ teaspoon finely ground sea salt

01 Cut the cauliflower head into quarters through the top, and cut out the core.

02 Rice it by putting it through the chute of a food processor fitted with the shredder blade. Alternately, use the coarse side of a box grater.

03 Heat a large skillet over medium-high heat and add the butter.

04 Add the cauliflower and salt and cook for 2 to 3 minutes, stirring often, until the cauliflower has softened a bit.

05 Serve hot, on its own or under any dish that has some sauce to soak up.

coconut cauli-rice

prep time: **5 minutes** | cook time: **10 minutes** | serves: **4**

My favorite Burmese restaurant in San Francisco serves coconut rice that is nothing short of out of this world. I resist the urge to do so, but I could easily eat an entire bowl of the stuff.

2 tablespoons shredded unsweetened coconut

1 large head cauliflower (about 2 pounds)

1 tablespoon coconut oil

1 cup full-fat coconut milk

½ teaspoon finely ground sea salt

2 tablespoons coconut butter

01 Preheat the oven to 350°F.

02 Toast the shredded coconut on a rimmed baking sheet for 3 to 4 minutes. Set aside.

03 Cut the cauliflower head into quarters through the top, and cut out the core.

04 Rice the cauliflower by putting it through the chute of a food processor fitted with the shredder blade. Alternately, use the coarse side of a box grater.

05 Melt the coconut oil in a large skillet over medium heat.

06 Add the cauliflower and sauté for 2 minutes or so, stirring constantly.

07 Add the coconut milk and salt and sauté another 5 minutes, or until the cauliflower is tender but not mushy.

08 Stir in the coconut butter and turn off the heat.

09 Serve sprinkled with the toasted coconut.

spanish cauliflower rice

prep time: **10 minutes** | cook time: **20 minutes** | serves: **4**

Back when I created cauliflower tortillas, I got the urge to make a Paleo super burrito. I created this recipe to stand in for the rice, but I loved it so much I ate half of it straight out of the pan with my tasting spoon. Make this as a side dish when you make tacos or fajitas. (Or just eat it straight from the pan, as I do.)

1 large head cauliflower (about 2 pounds)

1 tablespoon lard, light olive oil, or coconut oil

1 cup finely diced red onion (about 2 tiny)

1 teaspoon finely ground sea salt, divided

1 teaspoon ground coriander

½ teaspoon ground cumin

1 teaspoon dried oregano leaves

1 teaspoon minced garlic

1 cup finely diced tomatoes

¼ cup fresh cilantro leaves, chopped

1 tablespoon lime juice

handful of fresh cilantro leaves, for garnish (optional)

01 Cut the cauliflower head into quarters through the top, and cut out the core.

02 Rice the cauliflower by putting it through the chute of a food processor fitted with the shredder blade. Alternately, use the coarse side of a box grater.

03 Melt the lard in a large skillet over medium heat.

04 Add the onion and a pinch of the salt to the pan and sweat the onion for 8 to 10 minutes, or until very soft and translucent.

05 Add the coriander, cumin, oregano, garlic, and remaining salt and stir to combine. Add the cauliflower and sauté another 8 to 10 minutes, or until the cauliflower is soft. (Add a tablespoon of water if the spices begin to stick to the bottom of the pan.)

06 Turn off the heat and stir in the tomatoes and cilantro. Squeeze in the lime, give a quick stir, garnish with cilantro leaves, if desired, and serve.

scallion pine nut cauli-rice

prep time: **10 minutes** | cook time: **10 minutes** | serves: **4**

Rice at my mom's house was always a thing of beauty. Even with my years of restaurant experience, I never had success cooking it as perfectly as Mom. Hers was always absolutely flawless and never plain or boring. My favorite variation was her scallion pine nut rice, which took what was typically a boring side dish and made it worthy of center stage.

1 large head cauliflower (about 2 pounds)

3 tablespoons unsalted butter, duck fat, or preferred fat, divided

½ cup pine nuts

1 cup sliced scallions (about 1 bunch)

1 teaspoon finely ground sea salt

01 Cut the cauliflower head into quarters through the top, and cut out the core.

02 Rice the cauliflower by putting it through the chute of a food processor fitted with the shredder blade. Alternately, use the coarse side of a box grater.

03 Set a large skillet over medium heat and melt 2 tablespoons of the butter. Add the pine nuts. Stir constantly until they start to brown and become fragrant, about 2 minutes.

04 Add the scallions and sauté for 1 minute. Remove the pine nuts and scallions from the pan and set aside.

05 Set the pan back on medium heat and melt the remaining tablespoon of butter. Add the cauliflower and salt and sauté for 6 to 8 minutes, stirring often, until the cauliflower has softened a bit.

06 Stir in the scallions and pine nuts. Serve hot.

kale with cranberries, pecans, and caramelized onion

prep time: **10 minutes** | cook time: **1 hour** | serves: **4**

I'm always on a mission to find new ways to prepare kale. This version was definitely inspired by the fall season, when I have to resist the urge to put cranberries and pecans in almost everything.

1 medium onion, sliced into thin strips

1 tablespoon duck fat, light olive oil, unsalted butter, or preferred fat

½ cup raw pecans

2 bunches kale (about 1¼ pounds)

2 cloves garlic, sliced

½ teaspoon finely ground sea salt

½ cup dried cranberries

½ cup water, plus more as needed

01 Preheat the oven to 325°F.

02 Sauté the onion in a large skillet over medium heat with the fat for 10 minutes. Turn the heat down to medium-low and continue to cook until the onions are very soft and caramelized, about 40 minutes.

03 Meanwhile, toast the pecans: Place the pecans on a rimmed baking sheet and toast for 5 minutes in the oven.

04 Wash and stem the kale and tear into bite-sized pieces.

05 Once the onions are caramelized, add the kale, garlic, salt, and cranberries to the pan. Turn the heat up to medium and sauté for 5 minutes. Add the water and cover, steaming the kale for 5 minutes more, or until tender. Check the kale after 2 to 3 minutes to make sure the water hasn't all evaporated; if it has, add a bit more.

06 Toss with the toasted pecans and serve.

roasted green beans
with kalamata olive vinaigrette

prep time: **10 minutes** | cook time: **20 to 25 minutes** | serves: **4**

Until a few years ago, my go-to method of cooking string beans was stir-frying or sautéing on the stovetop. Ever since I roasted them, though, I'm a changed woman. In a hot oven, string beans get wonderfully caramelized while still maintaining their crunch. They're fantastic simply sprinkled with salt and pepper, but I also love to give them the full treatment; fatty olives, pungent garlic, and some brightness from the lemon rounds these out perfectly.

For the beans

1 pound green beans

6 cloves garlic, peeled and smashed with the flat side of a knife

2 tablespoons light olive oil or lard

¼ teaspoon sea salt

For the dressing

¼ cup pitted Kalamata olives, minced

2 tablespoons extra virgin olive oil

2 tablespoons minced fresh parsley (leaves from 4 to 6 sprigs)

1 teaspoon julienned lemon zest

1 tablespoon lemon juice

¼ teaspoon ground black pepper

01 Preheat the oven to 425°F.

02 Trim the stem ends off the green beans and toss them and the garlic cloves with the light olive oil and salt on a rimmed baking sheet. Roast for 20 to 25 minutes, giving them a shake after 10 minutes.

03 Meanwhile, make the dressing: Place the olives in a bowl with the extra virgin olive oil, parsley, lemon zest, lemon juice, and pepper.

04 Once the green beans are crisp-tender, toss them with half of the vinaigrette. Transfer to a platter and top with the remaining vinaigrette.

05 Serve warm or at room temperature.

chard with lemon and red pepper

prep time: **10 minutes** | cook time: **20 minutes** | serves: **4**

I love a good challenge, especially when it involves getting people to love vegetables. To my sweetie, Simon, all leafy greens taste bitter. He eats them because he knows they're good for him, but he doesn't love them. This chard dish was created solely with the intention of appealing to his palate. The first time I made these, I stared at him like a creeper from across the table when he took the first bite. "Well?! Are they bitter?" I asked. "Nope," he replied. Success!

2 bunches chard (green, red, or rainbow; about 1½ pounds)

2 tablespoons light olive oil or duck fat

1 large onion, thinly sliced

½ teaspoon finely ground sea salt

6 cloves garlic, thinly sliced

¾ cup Chicken Broth (page 128)

zest of 1 lemon, finely grated or cut into thin strips

2 tablespoons lemon juice

½ teaspoon red pepper flakes

01 Tear the chard leaves off the stems. Slice the stems into bite-sized pieces and roughly chop the leaves.

02 Heat the oil in a large skillet over medium-high heat. Add the sliced onion and chard stalks and sauté for 2 minutes, or until beginning to brown. Add the salt and turn the heat down to medium.

03 Sweat for another 8 to 10 minutes, stirring often. Add the garlic and cook for 1 more minute.

04 Add the broth, bring to a simmer, and place the greens on top. Once they're wilted enough to fold in (about 2 minutes), stir them into the onions.

05 Sauté for another 5 minutes, or until the chard is soft. If there is still liquid, turn the heat to high to reduce it.

06 Turn off the heat and stir in the lemon zest, lemon juice, and red pepper flakes. Serve hot.

double-bacon collard greens

prep time: **10 minutes** | cook time: **30 minutes** | serves: **4**

True southern collards are cooked with ham hocks for a good amount of time and get infused with plenty of salty, smoky goodness. This version, with apple cider vinegar, crispy bacon, and sweet onion, pays homage to that in a fraction of the time.

2 bunches collards (about 1½ pounds)

8 ounces bacon, divided

2 tablespoons finely ground sea salt

1 medium sweet onion, thinly sliced (Vidalia if available)

5 cloves garlic, thinly sliced

2 tablespoons apple cider vinegar

01 Cut off the bottom couple of inches of tough stems from the collards and discard. Stack up the leaves, roll them up, and slice crosswise into ½-inch-wide strips.

02 Put the collards into a large pot with one-quarter of the bacon and the salt. Cover with cold water.

03 Bring to a boil and cook for 10 to 12 minutes, or until the collards are bright green and soft. When soft, drain the collards and set aside. Discard the bacon they were cooked with.

04 Meanwhile, cut the remaining bacon into lardons (¼-inch strips) and cook in a large cast iron or stainless steel skillet over medium heat until crispy, about 10 to 15 minutes.

05 Remove the bacon and all but about 1 tablespoon of the fat from the pan. Drain the bacon on paper towels and reserve the extra fat for future use, if desired.

06 Add the sliced onion to the pan and cook over medium heat until golden brown and softened, about 10 minutes.

07 Add the garlic and cook for 1 minute more, stirring.

08 Add the apple cider vinegar to deglaze the pan. Scrape up any brown bits that have stuck to the bottom.

09 Add the collards and cook for another 3 minutes.

10 Remove to a serving platter and top with the crispy bacon.

sesame shiitake broccoli

prep time: **10 minutes** | cook time: **15 minutes** | serves: **4**

I hated broccoli as a kid. The only way I would eat it was if it was smothered in cheese or cooked in some kind of Asian sauce. The latter is still one of my favorite ways to prepare it, and the addition of shiitake mushrooms gives it an extra boost of umami goodness.

2 tablespoons coconut oil

8 ounces shiitake mushrooms, stemmed and halved

1½ pounds broccoli, cut into florets

1 (1-inch) piece fresh ginger, peeled and grated

¼ cup coconut aminos

¼ cup water

½ teaspoon finely ground sea salt

1 teaspoon black and/or white sesame seeds

01 Heat the oil in a large skillet or wok over medium-high heat.

02 Once the oil is shimmering, add the mushrooms and sauté for 1 to 2 minutes, or until they soften. Remove from the pan with a slotted spoon and set aside.

03 Add the broccoli to the pan and cook for 8 minutes, stirring occasionally, until browned and softened.

04 Add the ginger and cook another 2 minutes.

05 Add the coconut aminos, water, and salt and continue to cook for 2 to 3 minutes, or until the broccoli is crisp-tender.

06 Stir in the mushrooms and sesame seeds and serve.

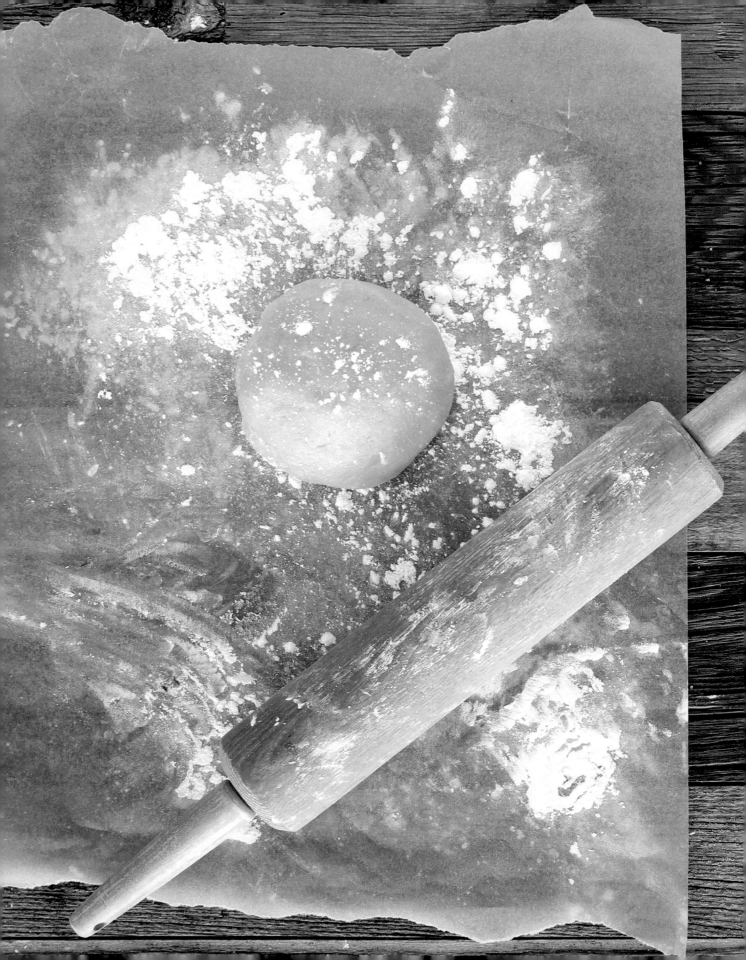

CRACKERS, WRAPS, AND BREADS

biscuits

prep time: **10 minutes** | cook time: **15 minutes** | makes: **10 to 12 biscuits**

Few things are as comforting as a warm, buttery, flaky biscuit. Few things are as versatile, too. These are equally wonderful as an accompaniment to Onion Eggs (page 76), as the base for Eggs Benedict (page 80), and as the "cake" in Strawberry Shortcake (page 268). Of course there's nothing wrong with simply slathering one with butter and enjoying it as a mid-afternoon snack, either.

2½ cups almond flour

¾ cup arrowroot powder

½ teaspoon finely ground sea salt

½ teaspoon baking soda

4 tablespoons cold unsalted butter, duck fat, or lard (see Note)

2 large eggs

2 tablespoons honey

01 Preheat the oven to 350°F and line a baking sheet with parchment paper.

02 In a large mixing bowl, combine the almond flour, arrowroot, salt, and baking soda. Stir with a whisk to combine.

03 Cut the butter into the dry ingredients with a pastry cutter or two knives. You want it to resemble coarse crumbs.

04 In a small bowl, beat the eggs and honey together and add to the dry ingredients.

05 Stir to combine.

06 Drop the batter onto the prepared baking sheet with a large spoon.

07 Bake for 12 to 15 minutes, or until cooked through and golden brown.

 Note: If you're using duck fat or lard, pop it in the freezer for 10 minutes to get it very cold.

pizza crust

prep time: **1½ hours** | cook time: **10 minutes** | makes: **1 (9- to 10-inch) crust**

What do you get when two New Yorkers have a baby? A pizza snob. To me, eating pizza with an inferior crust simply isn't worth it, and it just makes me crave the real thing even more. It's got to be crispy on the bottom and a little bit chewy. It's got to hold up to a pile of toppings but be delicious enough to hold its own with the lightest of toppings as well. I basically locked myself in the kitchen until I got this one right, and I can honestly say it was worth it. It has been a favorite on my blog ever since and has gotten the stamp of approval from thousands of Paleo New Yorkers.

▶ Make sure you have: parchment paper

1 tablespoon dry active yeast (naturally gluten-free, but check the package to be sure)

1 tablespoon honey

¼ cup warm water (should feel warm on the inside of your wrist but not burn)

1 tablespoon extra virgin olive oil (or other melted fat if you're opposed to heating olive oil)

1 tablespoon egg white (less than 1 egg)

1½ teaspoons apple cider vinegar

¾ cup almond flour

¾ cup tapioca starch

¾ teaspoon finely ground sea salt

01 In the warmed bowl of a stand mixer (or, alternatively, the bowl you'll be using with hand-held beaters), add the yeast, honey, and warm water and whisk to combine. Let sit for a good 5 minutes. It will get foamy and active. (If not, the yeast is a dud, and you'll need to start over.)

02 In a small bowl, combine the olive oil, egg white, and apple cider vinegar.

03 In a medium bowl, whisk to combine the almond flour, tapioca starch, and salt.

04 Once the yeast is foamy, add the wet and dry ingredients to the bowl with the yeast mixture and mix on medium-high for 30 seconds using the paddle attachment on a stand mixer, scraping down the bowl once to make sure it's all incorporated.

05 Scrape down the bowl with a rubber spatula again to gather the dough together. It will *not* look like the dough you remember; it is much wetter. Use the spatula to get it into as much of a ball as possible.

06 Cover the bowl with a tea towel and set in a warm (but not hot) place. Allow it to sit for 1¼ to 1½ hours. The dough won't rise as dramatically as a traditional dough recipe, but it will aerate and increase in size a bit.

07 After the dough has had time to rise, preheat the oven to 500°F. If using a pizza stone, place it in the oven to heat up while the oven preheats.

Note: Pre-cook toppings, such as meats and vegetables, that need longer than 2 to 3 minutes to cook.

08 Lightly oil a sheet of parchment paper and turn the dough out onto it. It will likely stick a bit to the bottom of the bowl; just scrape it out as best as you can.

09 With oiled hands, gently flatten out the pizza dough into a 9- to 10-inch circle. It will be aerated, so you might have to patch it together if there are empty spaces.

10 Carefully transfer the dough, still on the parchment, onto the pizza stone or a rimmed baking sheet.

11 Bake in the lower third of the oven for 6 to 8 minutes, or until it's starting to brown at the edges.

12 Add desired toppings and cook for 2 to 3 minutes more. Allow to cool for a minute before slicing.

bread sticks

prep time: **1½ hours** | cook time: **12 to 15 minutes** | makes: **10 bread sticks**

When I finally cracked the code for Paleo pizza crust, I felt like anything was possible. Sound dramatic? I'm actually trying to tone it down a bit. Even though the Paleo template shuns bread as a food group, I'm not buyin' it. If I can figure out a way to satisfy the need for crusty, chewy bread products, you better believe I'm going to do just that.

▸ Make sure you have: parchment paper

2 teaspoons dry active yeast (naturally gluten-free, but check the package to be sure)

1 tablespoon honey

¼ cup warm water (should feel warm on the inside of your wrist but not burn)

1 cup almond flour

½ cup arrowroot powder

1 tablespoon psyllium husks

¾ teaspoon finely ground sea salt

1 large egg

1 tablespoon light olive oil

1 tablespoon melted unsalted butter or light olive oil, for brushing

01 In the warmed bowl of your stand mixer (or, alternatively, the bowl you'll be using with hand-held beaters), add the yeast, honey, and warm water and whisk to combine.

02 In a medium bowl, whisk to combine the almond flour, arrowroot, psyllium husks, and sea salt.

03 Once the yeast is foamy, mix in the egg and olive oil, and then add the dry ingredients to the bowl and mix with the paddle attachment on medium-high for 30 seconds, scraping down the bowl once to make sure it's all incorporated.

04 Scrape down the bowl with a rubber spatula again to gather the dough together. It will *not* look like the dough you remember; it is much wetter. Use the spatula to get it into as much of a ball as possible.

05 Cover the bowl with a tea towel and set in a warm (but not hot) place. Allow it to sit for 1¼ to 1½ hours.

06 After 1¼ hours, check the dough to see if it's risen. It won't rise as dramatically as a conventional dough would, but it will have become aerated and gotten a bit larger.

07 Preheat the oven to 425°F.

Variation: Sea Salt–Studded Bread Sticks

Sprinkling these bread sticks with coarse sea salt adds some nice texture and flavor. Reduce the salt in the recipe to ½ teaspoon and sprinkle on some coarse sea salt after brushing with butter or oil before baking—just enough to get a crystal or two per bite.

08 Line a baking sheet with lightly oiled parchment paper.

09 Divide the dough into 10 sections and, with oiled hands, roll them into long skinny sticks. They will rise when cooked, so make them skinnier than you want the end result to be.

10 Transfer the sticks to the prepared baking sheet and brush with melted butter.

11 Bake for 12 to 15 minutes, or until they are golden brown.

plantain tortillas

prep time: **15 to 20 minutes** | cook time: **20 to 24 minutes** | makes: **12 to 16 small tortillas**

Most people think these are too good to be true until they make them. Made with a few simple ingredients, these babies wrap, roll, and hold all of the fillings your little heart desires. You can even make them gigantic for burritos. Be sure to use plantains that are just barely yellow; any riper than that and they'll still work, but they'll be on the sweet side.

▶ Make sure you have: parchment paper

3 to 4 yellow plantains (about 2 to 2 ½ pounds)

⅓ cup egg whites (2 to 3 large eggs)

3 tablespoons lard or fat of your choice, melted, plus more for greasing the parchment paper

½ teaspoon finely ground sea salt

1 teaspoon lime juice

 These store, freeze, and reheat beautifully. Reheat them over a gas flame for 20 seconds on each side, turning as needed, or in the oven or on a grill.

Although you may have to adjust the cooking time, you can make these any size you like.

01 Preheat the oven to 350°F.

02 Peel the plantains by cutting off the tops and bottoms and slicing through the skin along the length of the plantain.

03 Roughly chop the plantains and place in the bowl of a food processor or high-speed blender.

04 Add the egg whites, melted lard, salt, and lime juice. Blend until very smooth.

05 Line two baking sheets with parchment paper (or work in batches if you only have one).

06 Grease the parchment paper liberally.

07 Using a small ladle or disher, drop four ¼-cup portions of batter onto each pan, leaving plenty of room between each one.

08 Using the ladle and/or a rubber spatula, smooth out the batter into thin circles. Get them as thin as you can while still keeping them intact.

09 Bake for 10 to 12 minutes, or until they are dry to the touch and just starting to brown at the edges. If using two pans at once, switch halfway through.

10 Repeat with the remaining batter, making sure to grease the parchment paper each time.

basic crackers

prep time: **10 minutes** | cook time: **16 to 20 minutes** | makes: **about 50 crackers**

Crunch. While it's not a nutritional requirement, it could very well be considered a happiness requirement. When people go Paleo, it's often one of the first things they find themselves missing. And as a caterer, creating menus is a whole lot easier when I have a vehicle for delicious toppings. These crackers are about as versatile as it gets. They have a slight nutty flavor from the almond flour, but they are still neutral enough to let the toppings on them be the star. And of course, they're perfectly crispy and will hold their crunch for as long as they're around.

1 large egg (more if needed; see Note)

1 tablespoon extra virgin olive oil or melted butter

1½ cups almond flour

½ cup arrowroot powder

½ teaspoon finely ground sea salt

 Note: The size of the egg can have a pretty big impact on the texture of the dough. If it crumbles instead of coming together into a kneadable ball, beat another egg and add a little at a time until it does.

01 Preheat the oven to 350°F.

02 In a large mixing bowl, beat the egg with the olive oil.

03 Stir in the almond flour, arrowroot, and salt and mix until the dough comes together. Give it a knead or two to make sure it's well incorporated.

04 Roll the dough out in-between two sheets of parchment paper to a thickness of about ⅛ inch. Try and get it as close to a rectangle as possible.

05 Cut the dough into 1-inch squares with a sharp knife.

06 Slide the parchment and dough onto a baking sheet and bake for 10 to 12 minutes, or until the crackers begin to brown.

07 Turn the heat down to 325°F and bake for an additional 6 to 8 minutes, or until the crackers are crisp and light golden brown.

08 Remove from the oven and allow to cool before breaking the crackers apart.

09 Store in an airtight container.

rosemary crackers

prep time: **10 minutes** | cook time: **16 to 20 minutes** | makes: **about 50 crackers**

Fresh rosemary gives these crackers a lovely earthy flavor. Set them out with a cheese or charcuterie platter, or top them with prosciutto and fig jam for a simple and elegant hors d'oeuvre.

1 large egg (more if needed, see Note)

1 tablespoon extra virgin olive oil

1½ cups almond flour

½ cup arrowroot powder

1 tablespoon minced fresh rosemary

½ teaspoon finely ground sea salt

 Note: The size of the egg can have a pretty big impact on the texture of the dough. If it crumbles instead of coming together into a kneadable ball, beat another egg and add a little at a time until it does.

01 Preheat the oven to 350°F.

02 In a large mixing bowl, beat the egg with the olive oil.

03 Stir in the almond flour, arrowroot, rosemary, and salt and mix until the dough comes together. Give it a knead or two to make sure it's well incorporated.

04 Roll the dough out in-between two sheets of parchment paper to a thickness of about ⅛ inch. Try and get it as close to a rectangle as possible.

05 Cut the dough into 1-inch squares with a sharp knife.

06 Slide the parchment and dough onto a baking sheet and bake for 10 to 12 minutes, or until the crackers begin to brown.

07 Turn the heat down to 325°F and bake for an additional 6 to 8 minutes, or until the crackers are crisp and light golden brown.

08 Remove from the oven and allow to cool before breaking the crackers apart.

09 Store in an airtight container.

fig and olive crackers

prep time: **10 minutes** | cook time: **16 to 20 minutes** | makes: **about 50 crackers**

Fig and olive is one of my all-time favorite combinations. The honey-sweet figs are the perfect counterpoint to the briny, salty olives. For a truly sublime small bite, top these crackers with chevre, prosciutto, and a drizzle of raw honey.

1 tablespoon minced dried figs (about 3 small figs)

1 tablespoon minced Kalamata olives (about 4 olives)

1 egg (more if needed, see Note)

1 tablespoon extra virgin olive oil

1½ cups almond flour

½ cup arrowroot powder

⅛ teaspoon finely ground sea salt

 Notes: The size of the egg can have a pretty big impact on the texture of the dough. If it crumbles instead of coming together into a kneadable ball, beat another egg and add a little at a time until it does.

01 Preheat the oven to 350°F.

02 In a large bowl, whisk together the minced figs, minced olives, egg, and olive oil.

03 Stir in the almond flour, arrowroot, and salt.

04 Knead to combine.

05 Roll the dough out in-between two sheets of parchment paper to a thickness of about ⅛ inch. Try and get it as close to a rectangle as possible.

06 Cut the dough into 1-inch squares with a sharp knife.

07 Slide the parchment and dough onto a baking sheet and bake for 10 to 12 minutes, or until the crackers begin to brown.

08 Turn the heat down to 325°F and bake for an additional 6 to 8 minutes, or until the crackers are crisp and light golden brown.

09 Remove from the oven and allow to cool before breaking the crackers apart.

10 Store in an airtight container. Because of the moisture in the figs and olives, these crackers might need to be popped in the oven for 5 minutes to recrisp if you don't plan on serving them right away.

seeded crackers

prep time: **10 minutes** | cook time: **16 to 20 minutes** | makes: **about 50 crackers**

I will always have a soft spot in my heart for the iconic everything bagel. I created this cracker recipe to be reminiscent of that flavor. Top these with cream cheese (either dairy or cashew, page 68) and smoked salmon for an effortless crowd-pleaser.

1 large egg (more if needed, see Notes)

1 tablespoon extra virgin olive oil

¾ cup almond flour

½ cup arrowroot powder

¼ cup assorted seeds, such as sesame, caraway, black caraway, poppy (see Notes)

¼ teaspoon onion flakes

½ teaspoon finely ground sea salt

 Notes: The size of the egg can have a pretty big impact on the texture of the dough. If it crumbles instead of coming together into a kneadable ball, beat another egg and add a little at a time until it does.

I encourage you to use your favorite seeds in this recipe to make it your own. I love using about ⅛ cup sesame and filling in the remaining ⅛ cup with equal parts poppy, caraway, and black caraway. Black caraway seeds are also called *Nigella seeds* or *black cumin*. They have a slightly bitter, earthy flavor that adds a nice balance to this recipe. They can be found in Middle Eastern markets or online.

01 Preheat the oven to 350°F.

02 In a large mixing bowl, beat the egg with the olive oil.

03 Stir in the almond flour, arrowroot, seeds, onion flakes, and salt and mix until the dough comes together. Give it a knead or two to make sure it's well incorporated.

04 Roll the dough out in-between two sheets of parchment paper to a thickness of about ⅛ inch. Try and get it as close to a rectangle as possible.

05 Cut the dough into 1-inch squares with a sharp knife.

06 Slide the parchment and dough onto a baking sheet and bake for 10 to 12 minutes, or until the crackers begin to brown.

07 Turn the heat down to 325°F and bake for an additional 6 to 8 minutes, or until the crackers are crisp and light golden brown.

08 Remove from the oven and allow to cool before breaking the crackers apart.

09 Store in an airtight container.

DESSERTS

grandma's "dough" cookies

prep time: **10 minutes, plus 30 minutes to refrigerate** | cook time: **14 to 18 minutes** | makes: **about 3 dozen cookies**

When I was growing up, a few times a year we would get a shoebox full of cookies wrapped in the Jewish newspaper from my Grandma Helen. Among the cookies were her simple cut-out cookies, each of which had a single chocolate chip in the center. Once I realized the importance of holding on to old family recipes, I asked her how she made them. She looked at me as if I were asking how to make toast and said, in her cute Yiddish accent, "You make a dough."

1 egg

2 tablespoons unsalted butter or coconut oil, melted

1 tablespoon maple syrup

1½ cups almond flour

½ cup arrowroot powder

3 tablespoons coconut sugar

⅛ teaspoon finely ground sea salt

chocolate chips (optional)

01 In a large bowl, whisk together the egg, melted butter, and maple syrup.

02 With a wooden spoon, mix in the almond flour, arrowroot, coconut sugar, and salt. Knead with your hands to thoroughly combine.

03 Form the dough into a ball and wrap in plastic wrap. Refrigerate for at least 30 minutes.

04 Preheat the oven to 350°F. Line a baking sheet with parchment paper.

05 Roll out the chilled dough in-between two sheets of parchment paper to about ⅛ inch thick.

06 Cut into shapes with cookie cutters, or simply into squares if you prefer. Place a chocolate chip in the center, if desired.

07 Place the cookies on the prepared baking sheet, spacing about ½ inch apart, and bake for 14 to 18 minutes. They should be light golden brown and buttery when they're done. Allow to cool before serving.

 If you'd prefer to slice the cookies instead of rolling out the dough, form the dough into a log shape instead of a ball before wrapping in plastic wrap and refrigerating. Cut into ⅛-inch slices before baking.

lemon pound cake

prep time: **10 minutes** | cook time: **30 minutes** | makes: **1 (7½-by-3½-inch) loaf**

Lemon pound cake is one of those things that's just nice to have on hand. It's great with tea in the afternoon or for a light summer dessert with some raspberry sorbet spooned on top. (And I won't tell if you have it for breakfast.)

½ cup softened unsalted butter or palm shortening, plus more to grease the pan

¼ cup honey

4 large eggs

1 tablespoon finely grated lemon zest

2 tablespoons lemon juice

1¼ cups almond flour

¼ cup coconut flour

¼ cup arrowroot powder

1 teaspoon baking soda

¼ teaspoon finely ground sea salt

01 Preheat the oven to 350°F and grease a 7½-by-3½-inch loaf pan.

02 In a large bowl or the bowl to your stand mixer, beat together the butter, honey, eggs, lemon zest, and lemon juice until thoroughly combined.

03 In a medium bowl, sift together the almond flour, coconut flour, arrowroot, baking soda, and salt.

04 Pour the dry ingredients into the wet and beat on low just until incorporated.

05 Pour the batter into the prepared pan and bake for 25 to 30 minutes, or until a toothpick inserted in the center comes out clean.

 Variation: Lemon Poppy Cake
Add 2 tablespoons of poppy seeds to the dry ingredients.

berry custard tart

prep time: **1 hour (including time for dough to chill)** | cook time: **30 minutes** | makes: **1 (9-inch) tart**

I've always had a soft spot for those glazed fruit tarts that are in just about every bakery window. I loved how each one was different; there's a perfect fruit combination for everyone. Feel free to make these with whatever fruits you'd like, especially if there are wonderful ones in season.

For the crust

1 egg

2 tablespoons honey

2 tablespoons unsalted butter or coconut oil, melted

1½ cups almond flour

½ cup plus 2 tablespoons arrowroot powder

1 tablespoon coconut flour

⅓ teaspoon finely ground sea salt

For the pastry cream

1 tablespoon unflavored gelatin dissolved in 3 tablespoons water

1 (14-ounce) can full-fat coconut milk

2 egg yolks

¼ cup honey

2 teaspoons vanilla extract

For the berry topping

2 pints mixed berries (blueberries, raspberries, blackberries)

½ cup apricot jam (optional, see Note)

01 Preheat the oven to 350°F.

02 Make the crust: Whisk together the egg, honey, and melted butter in a large bowl.

03 With a wooden spoon, stir in the almond flour, arrowroot, coconut flour, and salt. Knead with your hands to combine, form into a disc, and refrigerate, wrapped tightly in plastic wrap, for 30 minutes.

04 Press into a 9-inch tart pan. Poke the bottom with a fork several times. Bake for 14 to 18 minutes, or until golden brown. Allow to cool.

05 Make the pastry cream: In a large bowl, sprinkle the gelatin over 3 tablespoons water and allow to soften.

06 In a medium saucepan, slowly heat the coconut milk until steaming. Place the egg yolks in a medium bowl and whisk well. Use a ladle to slowly pour in a small amount of the steaming milk, whisking constantly. Slowly pour the egg yolk and milk mixture back into the pan and continue whisking over low heat. Whisk constantly until thickened, about 10 minutes.

07 Place a fine-mesh strainer over the bowl with the gelatin and pour the coconut milk mixture through it. Whisk to dissolve the gelatin. Stir in the honey and vanilla and mix well.

08 Place the bowl inside a larger bowl with ice water in it. Stir until cool and thickened but still pourable.

Note: The apricot jam will create a shiny glaze on the berries and help hold them together when slicing, so they don't roll off quite as easily. However, it won't greatly affect the overall flavor of the tart.

09 To assemble: Once the custard and crust are cool, pour the custard into the tart crust. Arrange the berries on top.

10 If using, melt the apricot jam in a small saucepan, adding a few tablespoons of water if necessary. Strain to remove any pulp, return to the pan, and simmer for 5 minutes, or until slightly thickened.

11 Allow to cool a bit before gently applying the glaze to the fruit with a pastry brush. Store any leftovers in the fridge.

chocolate layer cake

prep time: **45 minutes** | cook time: **18 to 22** minutes | makes: **1 (9-inch) cake**

This cake recipe is based largely on the very popular No Joke Dark Chocolate Cake recipe that is on my blog. I've served it dozens of times to Paleo and non-Paleo folk alike, and it's gotten rave reviews every time. It is intensely chocolatey and not too sweet, and the texture is indistinguishable from regular chocolate cake.

For the cake

1½ cups almond flour

¾ cup arrowroot powder

¼ cup plus 2 tablespoons coconut flour

1½ teaspoons baking soda

¾ teaspoon salt

¾ cup cocoa powder

6 large eggs

1½ cups maple syrup

6 tablespoons melted unsalted butter or coconut oil, plus more for greasing the pans

1 tablespoon vanilla extract

For the chocolate whipped cream

6 ounces dark chocolate, chopped

3 tablespoons honey

3 tablespoons cocoa powder

1½ cups heavy cream or coconut cream (see Note)

 Note: If using coconut cream, put 2 to 3 (14-ounce) cans of full-fat coconut milk in the refrigerator the night before you plan to make the cake. Do not shake the cans! Open 2 of the cans and skim off the coconut cream that has risen to the top. You should get enough cream from 2 cans, but since the amount of fat varies in each can, it's a good idea to have a third as a backup, just in case.

01 Make the cake: Preheat the oven to 350°F and grease two 9-inch springform pans with butter or coconut oil.

02 Sift the almond flour, arrowroot, coconut flour, baking soda, salt, and cocoa powder into a large bowl.

03 In a medium bowl, whisk together the eggs, maple syrup, melted butter, and vanilla.

04 Add the wet ingredients to the dry and whisk until thoroughly combined.

05 Divide the batter between the two pans and bake for 18 to 22 minutes, or until the cakes spring back when you lightly touch the centers.

06 Cool completely in the pans on metal racks.

07 Make the chocolate whipped cream: Melt the chocolate in a double boiler over steaming water. Stir in the honey and cocoa powder, then remove from the heat and allow to cool.

08 Beat the cream or coconut cream in a stand mixer or with hand-held beaters until medium peaks form.

09 Slowly drizzle the melted chocolate into the cream, continuing to beat until well combined.

10 To assemble: Spread one-third of the whipped topping on the bottom layer of the cake. Set the second cake layer on top.

11 Cover the sides and top with the remaining whipped topping.

rustic apple tartlets

prep time: **30 minutes** | cook time: **30 minutes** | makes: **4 individual tartlets**

It has always been my understanding that the more difficult a pie crust is to work with, the better the end result will be. Consider that fair warning. It's certainly workable, but try not to get frustrated if it needs some patching while you work with it. Besides, the word *rustic* allows for a certain amount of character!

¾ pound apples (about 2), cut into half-moon slices ⅛ to ¼ inch thick

1 tablespoon coconut sugar, divided

1½ teaspoons plus ½ cup arrowroot powder, plus more for dusting

1½ teaspoons lemon juice

½ teaspoon ground cinnamon

1½ cups almond flour

pinch of finely ground sea salt

4 tablespoons cold unsalted butter

2 large eggs

1 teaspoon vanilla extract

01 In a medium mixing bowl, combine the sliced apples, 1½ teaspoons of the coconut sugar, 1½ teaspoons of the arrowroot, lemon juice, and cinnamon. Stir to combine and set aside.

02 In another bowl, whisk together the almond flour, remaining ½ cup of arrowroot, remaining 1½ teaspoons of coconut sugar, and the salt. Cut the butter into small pats and cut it into the dough with a pastry cutter or two knives.

03 Mix one of the eggs and the vanilla extract into the almond flour mixture. Keep mixing until it forms a dough.

04 Divide the dough into four even sections. On a floured piece of parchment paper, press each section into a disc. Dust the discs and a rolling pin with arrowroot and roll them out into circles about 5 inches across.

05 Beat the remaining egg in a small bowl and brush the tops of the discs. Slide the parchment and dough onto a baking sheet.

06 Arrange a row of apple slices in the center of each disc, leaving a space around the outside large enough to fold up.

07 Carefully fold up the sides of the discs around the outer edges of the apples. Using a flat metal spatula is helpful: Slide it under the dough and lift it up and over the apples, leaving the center uncovered. Using your fingers, crease the dough together every couple of inches to enclose the apples.

08 Brush the exposed apples with a little of the juice remaining in the bowl. Brush the crusts with the egg wash.

09 Bake for 25 to 30 minutes, or until the crust is golden and the apples have softened.

apple cider donut holes

prep time: **10 minutes** | cook time: **15 minutes** | makes: **25 to 30 donut holes**

Growing up in New England meant apple picking in the fall, and that meant big baskets of apple cider donuts at the orchard. Even though this version is grain-free, dairy-free, and nut-free, you'll be able to serve them to the masses without their having any idea that there's anything "missing."

1½ to 2 cups coconut or light olive oil, for frying

⅔ cup arrowroot powder

½ cup coconut flour

½ teaspoon baking soda

¼ teaspoon finely ground sea salt

4 large eggs

¼ cup honey

½ cup apple cider

⅓ cup coconut sugar or organic granulated sugar (see Note)

1 tablespoon ground cinnamon

 Note: Regular old cane sugar is the only thing that will provide that signature crunch that defines the apple cider donut, which is why I chose to include it as an option in this recipe—the only time you'll see it in this book. If you'd rather not use it, coconut sugar will still taste great, but it will have a different texture.

01 In a large saucepan, heat the oil to 360°F.

02 In a medium bowl, combine the arrowroot, coconut flour, baking soda, and salt. Whisk to combine.

03 In a large bowl, beat to combine the eggs, honey, and apple cider.

04 Pour the dry ingredients into the wet, and beat to combine.

05 Let rest for 1 minute. It will thicken a bit.

06 Once the oil is hot, carefully drop in a tablespoon of the dough at a time, trying to get the dough into the oil in one smooth motion. A disher is highly recommended for this, or use two spoons. Work in batches, frying 8 to 10 at a time.

07 With a long-handled slotted spoon, gently roll the donut holes once or twice until they're brown on all sides, about 3 to 4 minutes.

08 Remove with the slotted spoon to a wire rack placed over a rimmed baking sheet to drain.

09 Repeat with the remaining batter.

10 In a small bowl, combine the sugar and cinnamon. Shortly before you're ready to serve them, roll the donuts to coat.

brownies

prep time: **15 minutes** | cook time: **30 minutes** | makes: **1 dozen brownies**

Random fact: I didn't have a brownie made from a boxed mix until I was in college. The brownies of my childhood, like everything else, were made from scratch. I remember being sorely disappointed when I first tried an instant brownie. To me, the perfect brownie is dense, super chocolatey, and rich. These brownies are all of those things, and they're not only grain-free but nut-free, too!

1 cup unsalted butter or coconut oil, plus more to grease the pan

½ cup chocolate chips

½ cup honey

5 large eggs

1 cup coconut sugar, sifted

1 tablespoon vanilla extract

1 cup cocoa powder, sifted

¼ cup tapioca starch

1 tablespoon coconut flour

¼ teaspoon finely ground sea salt

01 Preheat the oven to 350°F. Grease a 9-by-13-inch baking pan.

02 Melt the butter and chocolate chips in a double boiler over simmering, not boiling, water. Remove from the heat and stir in the honey.

03 Using a stand mixer with the whisk attachment or a hand-held electric mixer, beat the eggs on medium-high speed until they're light yellow and fluffy. Add the coconut sugar, vanilla, and melted chocolate mixture. Beat on medium until well incorporated.

04 In a small bowl, whisk together the cocoa powder, tapioca starch, coconut flour, and salt. Add to the mixer and beat on low until smooth.

05 Pour the batter into the prepared pan and bake for 25 to 30 minutes, or until a toothpick inserted in the middle comes out clean. Allow to cool in the pan on a rack before cutting.

strawberry shortcake

prep time: **10 minutes, plus 1 hour for the berries to macerate** | serves: **4**

To me, this is the epitome of the ideal dessert: a barely sweet biscuit, freshly picked berries, and vanilla-spiked whipped cream. It doesn't get much better than that if you ask me, and it's one of the first things I make when berries start popping up at the farmers market in the spring.

2 cups fresh strawberries, sliced (or a combination of fresh berries)

1 tablespoon honey mixed with 2 tablespoons warm water

1 cup heavy cream or cream from a can of refrigerated full-fat coconut milk (see Note, page 260)

1 teaspoon vanilla extract, or 1 vanilla bean, scraped

4 Biscuits (page 240)

01 In a large, nonreactive bowl, mix together the berries and the honey-water mixture. Allow to sit for about 1 hour. The berries will release their juices and create their own sauce.

02 Beat the cream in a large bowl until soft peaks form. Mix in the vanilla.

03 Slice the biscuits in half and scoop one-fourth of the berry mixture and juice onto the bottom half. Top with whipped cream and the top half of the biscuit.

 If you prefer a sweeter, cakier base for your strawberry shortcake, use Lemon Pound Cake (page 256) instead of biscuits.

menus

Romantic Spring Dinner for Two

What's more romantic than cooking a beautiful dinner for the one you love? This menu is perfect for a stay-at-home Valentine's Day, or any day of the year that you want to treat your sweetie.

oysters rockefeller (page 96)

roasted beet and orange salad (page 114)

pistachio-crusted rack of lamb (page 184)

roasted asparagus (page 218)

strawberry shortcake (page 268)

Better than Takeout Feast

I don't know about you, but I miss Chinese delivery something fierce. While this spread won't exactly show up after making a phone call, the flavors are spot-on authentic. Even better: You won't have to worry about getting glutened! (Or soyed, or sugared, or MSGed, or cornstarched.)

hot and sour soup (page 130)

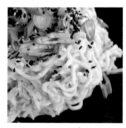

sesame zucchini noodles (page 212)

sesame shiitake broccoli (page 236)

twice-cooked pork belly (page 194)

ginger scallion pork meatballs (page 192)

orange-ginger beef stir-fry (page 202)

cauliflower rice (page 222)

Make-Ahead Dinner Party

Your guests will be blown away at the fact that you put together this impressive spread, but what they don't know is that everything on this menu can be made ahead and reheated when they arrive. Feel free to don an apron streaked with arrowroot powder and look like you've been slaving away all day, though. I won't tell.

roasted cauliflower soup with lime and pine nuts (page 136)

persimmon salad with grapes, prosciutto and almonds (page 116)

roasted sunchokes with rosemary salt (page 216)

crispy braised duck legs with melted shallots and roasted plums (page 168)

berry custard tart (page 258)

2 to 4 days before:

Make the soup (don't add garnishes until the day of).

Braise the duck legs and store them with their braising liquid.

Roast the sunchokes (don't sprinkle with rosemary salt until the day of).

1 day before:

Make the berry custard tart. Cover tightly and refrigerate until 2 to 3 hours before serving.

Day of:

• Prep the salad ingredients up to 2 hours before serving. Assemble salads shortly before your guests arrive.

• Roast the duck legs and the plums uncovered at 450°F for 15 to 20 minutes. Reheat the braising liquid in a small saucepan.

• Reheat the sunchokes at 450°F for 10 to 15 minutes. Sprinkle with rosemary salt before serving.

• Reheat the soup until hot and add the lime zest and pine nuts immediately before serving.

Summer Picnic

When the weather is perfect, it doesn't get much better than a big blanket stretched over the grass, a frosty glass of lemonade, and a basket full of delicious food.

summer salad with padron peppers (page 120)

grilled lemon-ginger chicken (page 172) (great cold!)

creamy purple cabbage slaw (page 126)

biscuits (page 240)

apple cider donut holes (page 264)

Fajita Party

How much fun is a huge spread of colorful, festive food complete with shells to wrap it all in? So much fun. Feel free to make some or all of the following suggestions, or make it potluck style and assign your friends a dish to bring.

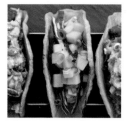
plantain tortillas (page 246)

coffee-rubbed flat iron fajitas (page 200)

cocoa-chili pork shoulder (page 190)

cilantro-lime roasted shrimp (page 150)

guacamole (page 48)

jicama slaw (page 124)

spanish cauliflower rice (page 224)

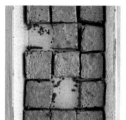
brownies (page 266) (You can add 1 teaspoon ground cinnamon and ¼ teaspoon cayenne pepper to give them a Mexican chocolate flavor!)

Giving Thanks

While turkey's great and all, I sometimes wish for a more adventurous Thanksgiving meal. This menu combines the flavors you love and remember with some new twists to amp it up a bit. For more Thanksgiving recipes, visit http://zenbellycatering.com/special-menus/thanksgiving/

kabocha squash and pomegranate salad (page 118)

roasted green beans with kalamata olive vinaigrette (page 230)

kale with cranberries, pecans, and caramelized onion (page 228)

whole roast duck with root vegetables and wild mushrooms (page 170)

rustic apple tartlets (page 262)

a glossary of cooking techniques

Braise: To cook low and slow with a moderate amount of liquid; often used for tougher cuts of meat.

Caramelize: To cook in fat over low heat, causing the sugars of the ingredient(s) to intensify.

Chiffonade: To cut very thin ribbons of herbs or leafy vegetables (see the illustrated step-by-step sequence on page 34).

Chop: Large, rough cuts, often used when the item in question will later be mashed or pureed, or is simply being used for flavor in a dish.

Deglaze: To add liquid to a hot pan to remove cooked-on residue. The browned bits in question are often from cooking meats and add great depth of flavor to a dish when released with a small amount of liquid. If you wind up scrubbing these off with a sponge instead, you missed an opportunity to elevate your dish!

Dice: Even, square cuts that can be either small (¼ inch), medium (½ inch), or large (1 inch). No need to break out a ruler here. The measurements are just meant to give you an idea. (See the illustrated step-by-step sequence for dicing an onion on page 32.)

Emulsify: To combine two ingredients that would normally be unblendable. This is done by slowly adding one (usually a fat) to the other and whisking constantly so that the two ingredients become smoothly blended. A third ingredient, often mustard or egg yolks, helps the process along and thickens the end result.

Julienne: Even, long, thin cuts. Often called "matchsticks."

Mince: To very finely dice; the smallest cut you can make with a knife.

Purée: To blend until smooth.

Reduce: To vigorously cook a liquid to evaporate some of the liquid and concentrate the flavors.

Roast: To cook with dry heat with a small amount of fat.

Sauté: To cook in fat on medium-high heat, to soften and brown.

Simmer: To bring a liquid to just below the boiling point, just barely bubbling.

Sweat: To cook on medium heat with salt, pulling the moisture out of the food without browning it.

recommended reading

Davis, William. *Wheat Belly: Lose the Wheat, Lose the Weight, and Find Your Path Back to Health*. Emmaus, PA: Rodale Books, 2011. (Author's site: http://www.wheatbellyblog.com)

CooksInfo.com (http://www.Cooksinfo.com)

Kresser, Chris. *Your Personal Paleo Code: The 3-Step Plan to Lose Weight, Reverse Disease, and Stay Fit and Healthy for Life*. New York: Little, Brown and Company, 2013. (Author's site: http://chriskresser.com)

Moore, Jimmy with Eric C. Westman, M.D. *Cholesterol Clarity: What the HDL Is Wrong with My Numbers?* Las Vegas: Victory Belt Publishing, 2013. (Author's site: http://www.livinlavidalowcarb.com)

Page, Karen, and Andrew Dorenburg. *The Flavor Bible*. New York: Little, Brown and Company, 2008. (Author's site: http://www.becomingachef.com)

Sanfilippo, Diane. *Practical Paleo: A Customized Approach to Health and a Whole-Foods Lifestyle*. Las Vegas: Victory Belt Publishing, 2012. (Author's site: http://balancedbites.com)

Sanfilippo, Diane. *The 21-Day Sugar Detox: Bust Sugar and Carb Cravings Naturally*. Las Vegas: Victory Belt Publishing, 2013. (Author's site: http://balancedbites.com)

Sanfilippo, Diane. *The 21-Day Sugar Detox Cookbook: Over 100 Recipes For Any Program Level*. Las Vegas: Victory Belt Publishing, 2013. (Author's site: http://balancedbites.com)

Sisson, Mark. *The Primal Blueprint: Reprogram your Genes for Effortless Weight Loss, Vibrant Health, and Boundless Energy*. Malibu: Primal Blueprint Publishing, 2013. (Author's site: http://marksdailyapple.com)

Wolf, Robb. *The Paleo Solution: The Original Human Diet*. Las Vegas: Victory Belt Publishing, 2010. (Author's site: http://robbwolf.com)

Wolfe, Liz. *Eat the Yolks: Discover Paleo, Fight Food Lies, and Reclaim Your Health*. Las Vegas: Victory Belt Publishing, 2013. (Author's site: http://realfoodliz.com)

conversion tables

3 teaspoons =
1 tablesoon =
½ ounce

2 tablespoons =
1 ounce =
⅛ cup

4 tablespoons =
2 ounces =
¼ cup

8 tablespoons =
4 ounces =
½ cup

16 tablespoons =
8 ounces =
1 cup

2 cups =
16 ounces =
1 pint

4 cups =
32 ounces =
1 quart

4 quarts =
1 gallon

acknowledgments

Mom: Pretty much any recipe I create is with the goal of getting it to taste as good as something you'd make. You are the most loving, thoughtful, and beautiful woman on the planet, and I'm a lucky girl to be have you as my mommy and biggest fan. I love you so much.

Simon: Shmoopers, you are my rock, my chief taste tester and dishwasher, and most importantly my comic relief. I could not have gotten through either starting a business or writing a book without your support and love. I know how much you love coming home to a clean house, and you are an extremely sweet man for putting up with the exact opposite of that for so many months. I adore you.

Elijah: I'm glad for you that you're getting out of the food biz, but I love nothing more than talking shop with you. Thanks for always being there to bounce ideas off of, and of course for being the best little brother on the planet.

Annabelle and Rowan: If I ever get to do *Chopped*, I'll be well prepared from all those practice rounds with you guys at dinner. Thanks for always keeping me on my toes, and for making me laugh until I snort.

Jen: Twenty-five years and going strong. Words cannot describe how grateful I am for your support and love. Ain't no mountain, girl.

Johnny: For laying the stones of the design of this book, and for creating such a beautiful cover: Thank you!

Friends in the Paleo community: I consider myself very fortunate to be part of such a supportive community of Paleo bloggers, business owners, and health professionals. While the atmosphere has the potential to be competitive, instead it is just the opposite, and that is a very wonderful thing. You know who you are, and I appreciate every one of you.

Erich, Michele, Holly, Susan, and Erin at Victory Belt: Thanks for always being there to field my long lists of questions, and for turning my vision of a book into something really beautiful.

My teachers: Saying I'm self-taught never quite feels right. I'm so grateful to you guys for all that I learned from you...

Deb and Rex: You hired a college student with an attitude and no professional cooking experience, and you taught me what it means to own a business and cook real food.

Samantha: I learned so much from you during my years at Simply Red—a whole lot about making excellent food, but mostly to be fearless.

*To me, life without veal stock, pork fat, sausage,
organ meat, demi-glace, or even stinky cheese is
a life not worth living.*

~ Anthony Bourdain

recipe thumbnail index

sauces, condiments, and basics

48 guacamole

50 avocado mousse

52 vinaigrettes

54 mayonnaise

56 dijon-herb aioli

57 garlic-dill aioli

58 rémoulade

60 stir-fry marinade and sauce

62 lemony hollandaise sauce

64 chimichurri

66 raita

68 cashew cream cheese

70 balsamic redux

eggs and breakfast

74 spinach, mushroom, and scallion frittata

76 onion eggs

78 silver dollar pancakes with blueberry compote

80 eggs benedict

82 loaded banana bread

84 blueberry muffins

86 apple spice muffins

88 chocolate hazelnut waffles

90 sweet cinnamon cereal

Starters, small bites, and party fare

94
chicken liver pâté

96
oysters rockefeller

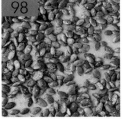
98
spiced pepitas

100
plantain shoestring fries

102
mango-chile ceviche

104
steak tartare

106
coconut shrimp with clementine-chili dipping sauce

108
maple-bourbon bacon jam

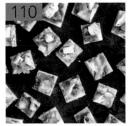
110
two-bite flatbreads

soups and salads

114
roasted beet and orange salad

116
persimmon salad with grapes, prosciutto, and almonds

118
kabocha squash and pomegranate salad

120
summer salad with padron peppers

122
raw kale salad with currants and pine nuts

124
jicama slaw

126
creamy purple cabbage slaw

128
rich chicken broth

130
hot and sour soup

132
bbq pork pho

134
chicken soup

136
roasted cauliflower soup with lime and pine nuts

138
tortilla soup

fish and seafood

142

grilled sardines

144

brazilian fish stew

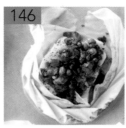
146

puttanesca fish en papillote

148

smoky roast salmon with cucumber tomatillo salsa

150

cilantro-lime roasted shrimp

152

thai green curry mussels

154

moules frites

poultry and rabbit

158

perfect roast chicken

160

citrus-herb spatchcock chicken

162

pan-roasted chicken with bacon and apples

164

crispy breaded cinnamon chicken fingers

166

roasted rabbit with grapes and pancetta

168

crispy braised duck legs with melted shallots and roasted plums

170

whole roast duck with root vegetables and wild mushrooms

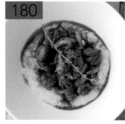
172

grilled lemon-ginger chicken

meat

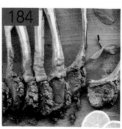
176

lamb curry

178

moroccan shepherd's pie

180

lamb stew with tomatoes, oranges, and olives

182

fresh herb lamb burgers with raita

184

pistachio-crusted rack of lamb

186
pork chops with stone fruit slaw

188
pork chops with caramelized apples

190
cocoa-chili pork shoulder

192
ginger scallion pork meatballs

194
twice-cooked pork belly

196
seared steaks with pan sauce

198
chili

200
coffee-rubbed flat iron fajitas

202
orange-ginger beef stir-fry

veggies and sides

206
cumin-orange roasted carrots

208
parsnip puree

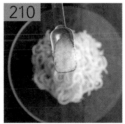
210
zucchini noodles

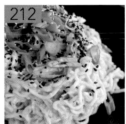
212
sesame zucchini noodles

214
spaghetti squash carbonara

216
roasted sunchokes with rosemary salt

218
roasted asparagus

220
best brussels

222
cauliflower rice

223
coconut cauli-rice

224
spanish cauliflower rice

226
scallion pine nut cauli-rice

228
kale with cranberries, pecans, and caramelized onion

230
roasted green beans with kalamata olive vinaigrette

232
chard with lemon and red pepper

234

double-bacon collard
greens

236

sesame shiitake
broccoli

crackers, wraps, and breads

240

biscuits

242

pizza crust

244

bread sticks

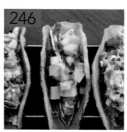
246

plantain tortillas

248

basic crackers

249

rosemary crackers

250

fig and olive crackers

251

seeded crackers

desserts

254

grandma's "dough"
cookies

256

lemon pound cake

258

berry custard tart

260

chocolate layer cake

262

rustic apple tartlets

264

apple cider donut holes

266

brownies

268

strawberry shortcake

index